COURSE EDITOR
Mrs. Chava Shapiro

AUTHORS
Mrs. Zeldy Friedman
Mrs. Chava Shapiro
Rabbi Michoel Shapiro

DIRECTORS OF CURRICULUM
Rabbi Mordechai Dinerman
Rabbi Naftali Silberberg

ROSH CHODESH SOCIETY DIRECTOR
Mrs. Shaindy Jacobson

PROJECT COORDINATORS
Mrs. Fraydee Kessler
Mrs. Rivki Mockin

BOOK DESIGN
Rabbi Zalman Abraham
Mendel Schtroks

Printed in the United States of America
© Published and Copyrighted 2016 by
The Rohr Jewish Learning Institute
822 Eastern Parkway, Brooklyn, NY 11213

(888) YOUR-JLI/718-221-6900
www.myJLI.com

SIMPLE TRUTHS

PIVOTAL JEWISH INSIGHTS FOR CENTERED LIVING

ROSHCHODESH *society*

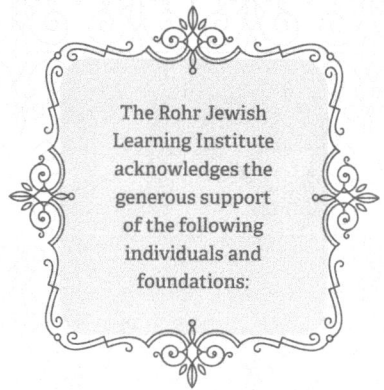

THE ROHR JEWISH LEARNING INSTITUTE

gratefully acknowledges
the pioneering support of

GEORGE AND PAMELA ROHR

Since its inception,
the Rohr JLI has been
a beneficiary of the vision, generosity,
care, and concern
of the Rohr family.

In the merit of
the tens of thousands of hours of Torah study
by JLI students worldwide,
may they be blessed with health,
Yiddishe nachas from all their loved ones,
and extraordinary success
in all their endeavors.

DEDICATED BY

Myrna Zisman

in loving memory of her dear husband

Leibel (Leo) Zisman

ר' אריה לייב בן שרגא פייוול ז"ל

As a survivor, Leibel's life was committed to building.

Out of destruction, was born a life of construction.

Leibel was a builder by profession, but his real passion lay in building his family, his community, and his people, fueled by his devotion to the Rebbe.

May the light of Torah and Judaism kindled by the Rosh Chodesh Society chapters across the globe bring eternal merit to his soul and may his memory be for a blessing.

———

חכמות נשים בנתה ביתה
משלי יד, א

"The wise woman builds her home."
—Proverbs 14:1

As Leibel's beloved and trusted life partner, Myrna imbues her home with warmth, love, light, and kindness.

May her merits never cease.

May she go from strength to strength, and enjoy health, happiness, nachas from her loved ones, and success in all her endeavors.

TABLE OF CONTENTS

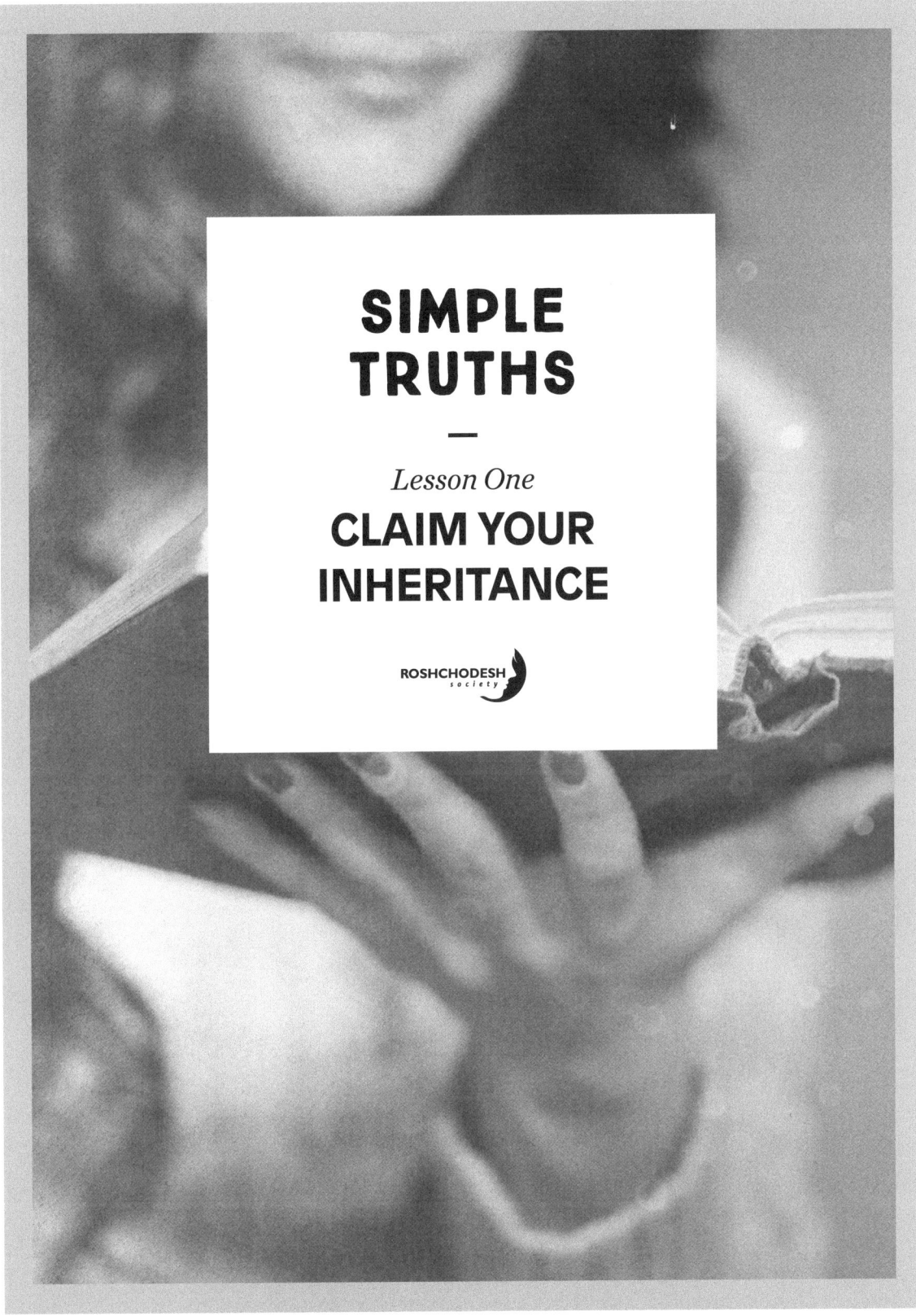

COURSE INTRODUCTION

Question for Discussion

Imagine you had the task of compiling several concepts from the Torah and the Jewish holy books that encapsulate the most foundational and transformative ideas in Judaism. What would you choose?

Figure 1.1

The Twelve Torah Texts

1) DEUTERONOMY 33:4

תּוֹרָה צִוָּה לָנוּ מֹשֶׁה
מוֹרָשָׁה קְהִלַּת יַעֲקֹב.

Torah tsivah lanu Moshe,
morashah kehilat Ya'akov.

The Torah that Moses commanded us is the heritage of the Congregation of Jacob.

2) DEUTERONOMY 6:4

שְׁמַע יִשְׂרָאֵל ה׳
אֱלֹקֵינוּ ה׳ אֶחָד.

Shema Yisrael, Ado-nai
Elo-heinu, Ado-nai echad.

Hear O Israel, the Lord is our God, God is One.

3) TALMUD, PESACHIM 116B

בְּכָל דּוֹר וָדוֹר חַיָּב אָדָם לִרְאוֹת אֶת
עַצְמוֹ כְּאִלּוּ הוּא יָצָא מִמִּצְרָיִם.

Bechol dor vador chayav adam lirot et
atsmo ke'ilu hu yatsa mimitsrayim.

In every generation every person must see oneself as if he or she had personally left Egypt.

4) TALMUD, SANHEDRIN 90A

כָּל יִשְׂרָאֵל יֵשׁ לָהֶם חֵלֶק לְעוֹלָם
הַבָּא, שֶׁנֶּאֱמַר: "וְעַמֵּךְ כֻּלָּם
צַדִּיקִים לְעוֹלָם יִירְשׁוּ אָרֶץ, נֵצֶר
מַטָּעַי מַעֲשֵׂה יָדַי לְהִתְפָּאֵר".

Kol yisrael yesh lahem chelek
le'olam haba, shene'emar, ve'amech kulam
tsadikim, le'olam yirshu arets, netser
mata'ai, ma'aseh yadai lehitpa'er.

All of Israel has a share in the World to Come, as it is stated (Isaiah 60:21): "Your people are all righteous; they shall forever inherit the land. They are the branch of My planting, the work of My hands, in which I take pride."

5) DEUTERONOMY 30:14

כִּי קָרוֹב אֵלֶיךָ הַדָּבָר מְאֹד,
בְּפִיךָ וּבִלְבָבְךָ לַעֲשֹׂתוֹ.

Ki karov elecha hadavar me'od
beficha uvilvavcha la'asoto.

It is close to you [i.e., within your reach to] follow
the Torah in speech, feeling, and deed.

6) TANYA, CHAPTER 41

וְהִנֵּה ה' נִצָּב עָלָיו וּמְלֹא כָל
הָאָרֶץ כְּבוֹדוֹ, וּמַבִּיט עָלָיו וּבוֹחֵן
כְּלָיוֹת וָלֵב, אִם עוֹבְדוֹ כָּרָאוּי.

Vehinei Hashem nitsav alav umelo chol
ha'arets kevodo, umabit alav uvochen
kelayot valev im ovdo kara'uy.

God stands above you, and [though] the whole earth
is full of His glory, He searches *your* mind and heart
to see whether you are serving Him properly.

7) GENESIS 1:1

בְּרֵאשִׁית בָּרָא אֱלֹקִים אֵת
הַשָּׁמַיִם וְאֵת הָאָרֶץ.

Bereishit bara Elo-him et
hashamayim ve'et ha'arets.

In the beginning, God created the heavens and the earth.

8) DEUTERONOMY 6:7

וְשִׁנַּנְתָּם לְבָנֶיךָ וְדִבַּרְתָּ בָּם,
בְּשִׁבְתְּךָ בְּבֵיתֶךָ וּבְלֶכְתְּךָ
בַדֶּרֶךְ וּבְשָׁכְבְּךָ וּבְקוּמֶךָ.

Veshinantam levanecha vedibarta bam,
beshivtecha beveitecha uvelechtecha
vaderech uveshochbecha uvekumecha.

You shall diligently teach [the Torah] to your children, and you
should speak [words of Torah] when you are home and when you
travel, before you lie down to sleep and when you wake up.

9) TALMUD, MEGILAH, 6B

יָגַעְתִּי וְלֹא מָצָאתִי – אַל תַּאֲמִין.   Yagati velo matsati al ta'amin.

לֹא יָגַעְתִּי וּמָצָאתִי – אַל תַּאֲמִין.   Lo yagati umatsati al ta'amin.

יָגַעְתִּי וּמָצָאתִי תַּאֲמִין.   Yagati umatsati ta'amin.

If someone says, "I worked hard, yet I have not succeeded," don't believe this person. If someone says, "I have not worked hard, yet I have succeeded," don't believe this person. If someone says, "I have worked hard, and I have succeeded," believe this person.

10) JERUSALEM TALMUD, NEDARIM 9:4

"וְאָהַבְתָּ לְרֵעֲךָ כָּמוֹךָ" – רַבִּי עֲקִיבָא   Ve'ahavta lere'acha kamocha. Rabi Akiva

אוֹמֵר, "זֶה כְּלָל גָּדוֹל בַּתּוֹרָה".   omer, zeh klal gadol baTorah.

"Love your fellow as yourself" (Leviticus 19:18). Rabbi Akiva says this is a great principle of the Torah.

11) TANYA, CHAPTER 33

וְזֶה כָּל הָאָדָם וְתַכְלִית בְּרִיאָתוֹ וּבְרִיאַת   Vezeh kol ha'adam vetachlit bri'ato uvri'yat

כָּל הָעוֹלָמוֹת, עֶלְיוֹנִים וְתַחְתּוֹנִים,   kol ha'olamot elyonim vetachtonim,

לִהְיוֹת לוֹ יִתְבָּרֵךְ דִּירָה זוֹ בְּתַחְתּוֹנִים.   lih'yot lo yitbarach dirah zo betachtonim.

The purpose of the creation of every human being and of all the worlds is for God to have a home in this lowly realm.

12) TANYA, CHAPTER 33

יִשְׂמַח יִשְׂרָאֵל בְּעוֹשָׂיו, פֵּרוּשׁ:   Yismach Yisrael be'osav, perush

שֶׁכָּל מִי שֶׁהוּא מִזֶּרַע יִשְׂרָאֵל יֵשׁ   shekol mi shehu mizera Yisrael yesh

לוֹ לִשְׂמֹחַ בְּשִׂמְחַת ה', אֲשֶׁר שָׂשׂ   lo lismo'ach besimchat Hashem asher sas

וְשָׂמֵחַ בְּדִירָתוֹ בְּתַחְתּוֹנִים.   vesame'ach bedirato betachtonim.

"Israel should rejoice in its Maker" (Psalms 149:2). Every member of Israel ought to share in God's joy and happiness, which He derives from His dwelling place in this lowly realm.

LESSON INTRODUCTION

Questions for Discussion

1. When you hear the word "religion," what comes to mind?

2. When you hear the word "Torah," what comes to mind?

3. Religion is defined in the Oxford Dictionary as "the belief in and worship of a superhuman controlling power, especially a personal God or gods." Does this definition resonate with you as describing Judaism?

THE ODD JEWISH OBSESSION

Text 1
RABBI MAURICE LAMM – "GOT TORAH?"

No word in the Jewish religion is so indefinable and yet so indispensable as the word Torah. Torah is the most comprehensive term for the substance of Judaism. Torah is Teaching. Torah is Law. No one can hope to achieve even a minimal appreciation of the Jewish religion without learning, and then reflecting on, the idea of Torah and its place in the life of the Jew. . . . For ages, Torah has been the sum and substance of Jewish scholarship. But it would be utterly wrong to conclude from this emphasis on study that Jewish spirituality runs dry in the sands of intellectualism. . . .

Photo archives from the Warsaw ghetto show a door of an inn that read, "Society of Wagon Drivers for the Study of Talmud in Warsaw." This referred to coachmen who seized a few moments from their work to gather in a group to "nosh" (grab a tasty morsel of) a page of Talmud. . . . These were not intellectuals, concerned only with the intricacies of scholastic dialectics; they were deeply religious men thirsting for spiritual refreshment and they found it, as countless generations of Jews before them, in the study of Torah.

"Oh, how I love Thy Torah; it is my meditation all day long" (Psalms 119:97). With Torah understood in its fullest sense, this may be taken as the

RABBI MAURICE LAMM

Congregational rabbi and noted author. Rabbi Lamm is the author of *The Jewish Way in Death and Mourning* and *The Jewish Way in Love and Marriage*. He was the rabbi of Beth Jacob of Beverly Hills from 1972–1985. He is president of the National Institute for Jewish Hospice and professor at Yeshiva University's rabbinical seminary in New York.

authentic attitude of the believing Jew to Torah. Torah is law, but it is much, much more than law.

Text 2

SIDDUR, MORNING BLESSINGS, CITED FROM TALMUD, SHABBAT 127A

אֵלּוּ דְבָרִים שֶׁאָדָם אוֹכֵל פֵּרוֹתֵיהֶם בָּעוֹלָם הַזֶּה וְהַקֶּרֶן קַיֶּמֶת לוֹ לָעוֹלָם הַבָּא, וְאֵלּוּ הֵן: כִּבּוּד אָב וָאֵם, וּגְמִילוּת חֲסָדִים, וְהַשְׁכָּמַת בֵּית הַמִּדְרָשׁ שַׁחֲרִית וְעַרְבִית, וְהַכְנָסַת אוֹרְחִים, וּבִקּוּר חוֹלִים, וְהַכְנָסַת כַּלָּה, וְהַלְוָיַת הַמֵּת, וְעִיּוּן תְּפִלָּה, וַהֲבָאַת שָׁלוֹם בֵּין אָדָם לַחֲבֵרוֹ וּבֵין אִישׁ לְאִשְׁתּוֹ. וְתַלְמוּד תּוֹרָה כְּנֶגֶד כֻּלָּם.

These are the *mitzvot*, the fruits of which we enjoy in this world, while the principal reward remains in the World to Come: honoring one's father and mother, performing deeds of kindness, early attendance at the House of Study morning and evening, hospitality, visiting the sick, providing the needs of a bride, escorting the dead, focus in prayer, bringing peace between man and his fellow and between husband and wife. And the study of Torah is equivalent to them all combined.

Question for Discussion

Why do you think Torah study is considered equivalent to all these *mitzvot* combined?

Text 3

MAIMONIDES, *MISHNEH TORAH*, LAWS OF TORAH STUDY 1:8

כָּל אִישׁ מִיִּשְׂרָאֵל חַיָּיב בְּתַלְמוּד תּוֹרָה, בֵּין עָנִי בֵּין עָשִׁיר, בֵּין שָׁלֵם בְּגוּפוֹ בֵּין בַּעַל יִסּוּרִין, בֵּין בָּחוּר בֵּין שֶׁהָיָה זָקֵן גָּדוֹל שֶׁתָּשֵׁשׁ כֹּחוֹ. אֲפִילוּ הָיָה עָנִי הַמִּתְפַּרְנֵס מִן הַצְּדָקָה וּמְחַזֵּר עַל הַפְּתָחִים וַאֲפִילוּ בַּעַל אִשָּׁה וּבָנִים חַיָּיב לִקְבּוֹעַ לוֹ זְמַן לְתַלְמוּד תּוֹרָה בַּיּוֹם וּבַלַּיְלָה, שֶׁנֶּאֱמַר (יְהוֹשֻׁעַ א, ח) "וְהָגִיתָ בּוֹ יוֹמָם וָלַיְלָה".

Every Jew is obligated to study Torah, whether poor or rich, healthy or ill, young or old. Even a pauper who derives his livelihood from charity, or if he has family obligations to his wife and children, must still establish fixed times for Torah study—both day and night, as it says (Joshua 1:8), "You shall contemplate it day and night."

RABBI MOSHE BEN MAIMON (MAIMONIDES, RAMBAM)
1135–1204

Halachist, philosopher, author, and physician. Maimonides was born in Cordoba, Spain. After the conquest of Cordoba by the Almohads, he fled Spain and eventually settled in Cairo, Egypt. There, he became the leader of the Jewish community and served as court physician to the vizier of Egypt. He is most noted for authoring the *Mishneh Torah*, an encyclopedic arrangement of Jewish law, and for his philosophical work, *Guide for the Perplexed*. His rulings on Jewish law are integral to the formation of halachic consensus.

Text 4

TALMUD, SUKAH 42A

יוֹדֵעַ לְדַבֵּר אָבִיו לוֹמְדוֹ תּוֹרָה וּקְרִיאַת שְׁמַע. תּוֹרָה מַאי הִיא?
אָמַר רַבִּי הַמְנוּנָא, "תּוֹרָה צִוָּה לָנוּ מֹשֶׁה מוֹרָשָׁה קְהִילַת יַעֲקֹב"
(דְּבָרִים לג, ד).

When a child learns to speak, the father teaches the child Torah and how to recite the *Shema*. What Torah does he teach? "The Torah that Moses commanded us is the inheritance of the congregation of Jacob" (Deuteronomy 33:4).

BABYLONIAN TALMUD

A literary work of monumental proportions that draws upon the legal, spiritual, intellectual, ethical, and historical traditions of Judaism. The 37 tractates of the Babylonian Talmud contain the teachings of the Jewish sages from the period after the destruction of the 2nd Temple through the 5th century CE. It has served as the primary vehicle for the transmission of the Oral Law and the education of Jews over the centuries; it is the entry point for all subsequent legal, ethical, and theological Jewish scholarship.

Figure 1.2

The Primacy of Torah Study

1   Torah study is considered equivalent in importance to all other *mitzvot* combined.

2   Every Jew must study Torah, regardless of age, stage, profession, or intellectual capacity.

3   The importance of Torah is the first value a Jewish parent instills in a child.

Questions for Discussion

Why do you think Judaism places so much emphasis on study? Does this enchantment with Torah study resonate with you?

THE ULTIMATE GUIDE FOR LIFE

Text 5

MAIMONIDES, *MISHNEH TORAH*, LAWS OF TORAH STUDY 3:3

אֵין לְךָ מִצְוָה בְּכָל הַמִּצְוֹת כּוּלָן שֶׁהִיא שְׁקוּלָה כְּנֶגֶד תַּלְמוּד
תּוֹרָה, אֶלָּא תַּלְמוּד תּוֹרָה כְּנֶגֶד כָּל הַמִּצְוֹת כּוּלָן. שֶׁהַתַּלְמוּד
מֵבִיא לִידֵי מַעֲשֶׂה.

There is no mitzvah that is equal to Torah study. Rather, Torah study is equal to all the *mitzvot*. This is because study leads to mitzvah performance.

Text 6

PROVERBS 8:35

כִּי מֹצְאִי מָצָא חַיִּים.

He who has found me [Torah] has found life.

Text 7

DEUTERONOMY 6:7

וְשִׁנַּנְתָּם לְבָנֶיךָ וְדִבַּרְתָּ בָּם, בְּשִׁבְתְּךָ בְּבֵיתֶךָ וּבְלֶכְתְּךָ בַדֶּרֶךְ וּבְשָׁכְבְּךָ וּבְקוּמֶךָ.

You shall diligently teach [the Torah] to your children, and you should speak [words of Torah] when you are home and when you travel, before you lie down to sleep and when you wake up.

Figure 1.3

Level 1: Guide for Our Lives

Torah's wisdom guides us in every facet of our lives. Studying Torah helps us reach our full potential.

ULTIMATE ONENESS
WILL AND WISDOM

Text 8
PROVERBS 8:30

וָאֶהְיֶה אֶצְלוֹ אָמוֹן, וָאֶהְיֶה שַׁעֲשֻׁעִים יוֹם יוֹם מְשַׂחֶקֶת לְפָנָיו בְּכָל עֵת.

I [the Torah] was raised at His side. I was His constant delight, and I always rejoiced in His presence.

ABSOLUTE ONENESS

Text 9a
EXODUS 20:2

אָנֹכִי ה' אֱלֹקֶיךָ אֲשֶׁר הוֹצֵאתִיךָ מֵאֶרֶץ מִצְרַיִם מִבֵּית עֲבָדִים.

I [anochi] am your God, Who took you out of Egypt, from the house of slavery.

Text 9b

TALMUD, SHABBAT 105A

"אָנֹכִי", נוֹטָרִיקוֹן: "אֲנָא נַפְשִׁי כְּתָבִית יְהָבִית".

The word *anochi* is an acronym for the words: *ana nafshi ketavit yehavit*, "I have written Myself into [this Torah] and given it [to you]."

Text 10

RABBI SHNE'UR ZALMAN OF LIADI, *TANYA*, CH. 4

RABBI SHNE'UR ZALMAN OF LIADI (ALTER REBBE)
1745–1812

Chasidic rebbe, halachic authority, and founder of the Chabad movement. The Alter Rebbe was born in Liozna, Belarus, and was among the principal students of the Magid of Mezeritch. His numerous works include the *Tanya*, an early classic containing the fundamentals of Chabad Chasidism, and *Shulchan Aruch HaRav*, an expanded and reworked code of Jewish law.

כְּמוֹ שֶׁכָּתוּב בְּזֹהַר, דְּאוֹרַיְיתָא וְקוּדְשָׁא בְּרִיךְ הוּא כּוּלָּא חַד. פֵּירוּשׁ: דְּאוֹרַיְיתָא, הִיא חָכְמָתוֹ וּרְצוֹנוֹ שֶׁל הַקָּדוֹשׁ בָּרוּךְ הוּא, וְהַקָּדוֹשׁ בָּרוּךְ הוּא בִּכְבוֹדוֹ וּבְעַצְמוֹ כּוּלָּא חַד, כִּי "הוּא הַיּוֹדֵעַ וְהוּא הַמַּדָּע וְכוּ'", כְּמוֹ שֶׁנִּתְבָּאֵר לְעֵיל בְּשֵׁם הָרַמְבַּ"ם.

The Zohar explains that the Torah and the Holy One, blessed be He, are one. This means that the Torah—which is God's wisdom and will—is one with God's Essence, since, in the words of Maimonides, "He is both the Knower and the knowledge."

Figure 1.4

Level 1: Guide for Our Lives

Torah's wisdom guides us in every facet of our lives. Studying Torah helps us reach our full potential.

Level 2: Oneness with God

Torah is God's will and wisdom, which He shares with us. Because God is one with the Torah, by studying Torah, we become one with Him.

CONCLUSION—
TWO SIMPLE TRUTHS
TORAH IS OURS

Text 11

RABBI SHNE'UR ZALMAN OF LIADI, *TANYA*, CH. 40

וּמִי . . . [שֶׁ]נַפְשׁוֹ שׁוֹקֵקָה וּצְמֵאָה לַה' וְכָלְתָה אֵלָיו כָּל הַיּוֹם
וְאֵינוֹ מְרַוֶּה צִמְאוֹנוֹ בְּמֵי הַתּוֹרָה שֶׁלְּפָנָיו, הֲרֵי זֶה כְּמִי שֶׁעוֹמֵד
בְּנָהָר וְצוֹעֵק, "מַיִם! מַיִם לִשְׁתּוֹת!" כְּמוֹ שֶׁקּוֹבֵל עָלָיו הַנָּבִיא,
"הוֹי כָּל צָמֵא לְכוּ לַמַּיִם" (יְשַׁעְיָהוּ נה, א).

One . . . whose soul yearns and thirsts for God and longs for Him all day, yet does not quench this thirst with the readily available "waters of the Torah," is like one who stands in a river and cries: "Water! [I need] water to drink!" The prophet thus laments over such a person [and proclaims]: "Come, all who thirst, and go to the waters" (Isaiah 55:1).

WE MUST WORK TO CLAIM IT

Text 12

SIDDUR, BLESSINGS BEFORE THE *SHEMA*

אָבִינוּ אָב הָרַחֲמָן, הַמְרַחֵם, רַחֵם נָא עָלֵינוּ. וְתֵן בְּלִבֵּנוּ בִּינָה,
לְהָבִין וּלְהַשְׂכִּיל, לִשְׁמֹעַ לִלְמֹד וּלְלַמֵּד, לִשְׁמֹר וְלַעֲשׂוֹת וּלְקַיֵּם
אֶת כָּל דִּבְרֵי תַלְמוּד תּוֹרָתֶךָ בְּאַהֲבָה.
וְהָאֵר עֵינֵינוּ בְּתוֹרָתֶךָ, וְדַבֵּק לִבֵּנוּ בְּמִצְוֹתֶיךָ, וְיַחֵד לְבָבֵנוּ
לְאַהֲבָה וּלְיִרְאָה אֶת שְׁמֶךָ.

Our Father, merciful Father Who is compassionate, have mercy on us! Grant our hearts understanding to comprehend and to discern, to listen, to learn and to teach, to observe, to practice, and to lovingly fulfill all the teachings of Your Torah.

Enlighten our eyes in Your Torah, cause our hearts to hold fast to Your commandments, and unify our hearts to love and revere Your Name.

My Personal Take

In the space provided below, write down, in your own words, the two simple truths you learned in today's lesson.

תּוֹרָה צִוָּה לָנוּ
מֹשֶׁה מוֹרָשָׁה
קְהִלַּת יַעֲקֹב.

The Torah that Moses commanded us is the heritage of the Congregation of Jacob.

וְשִׁנַּנְתָּם
לְבָנֶיךָ וְדִבַּרְתָּ
בָּם, בְּשִׁבְתְּךָ
בְּבֵיתֶךָ וּבְלֶכְתְּךָ
בַדֶּרֶךְ וּבְשָׁכְבְּךָ
וּבְקוּמֶךָ.

You shall diligently teach [the Torah] to your children, and you should speak [words of Torah] when you are home and when you travel, before you lie down to sleep and when you wake up.

Writing/Take-Home Exercise

Write down a subject or part of Torah (e.g., weekly Torah portion, the laws of *kashrut*) that you wish to learn, and set a goal as to how often you will learn this subject in the next month. Pair up with someone in the class—your *chavruta*—with whom you will learn this subject.

Key Points

1. Torah study holds an exalted place in Jewish life. We study all parts of Torah—even those which have seemingly little relevance to our lives—with equal passion and zeal, for the Torah's value runs deeper than being a rule book or guide to ritual observance.

2. Torah is a guidebook for *life*—its teachings illuminate and inspire all aspects of our lives, teaching us how to attain happiness and success, and reach our utmost potential.

3. Torah is God's essential will and wisdom. In giving us the Torah, God shared with us His most essential desires and how He thinks. When we study Torah, we spiritually "ingest" and absorb this divine information.

4. God's will and wisdom are not separate from God Himself, but are one with Him. Torah may look like wisdom, but it's essentially God Himself—wisdom is only the disguise, the packaging. Therefore, through learning Torah, we experience the ultimate intimacy and oneness with God.

5. Connecting with God is a deep-seated need and longing of every Jew. This thirst for God can be fully quenched only through Torah study.

6. While Torah is our birthright, we must also work to make it ours and to ensure that it continues to thrive through the generations. We do this through studying it and cherishing it, and by ensuring that we provide our children with a Torah education.

7. While the father has the legal obligation to ensure his children receive a formal Torah education, the mother ensures that her children are imbued with an understanding of the specialness and beauty of Torah.

APPENDICES

Appendix A
TALMUD, BERACHOT 61B

Once, the wicked government [of Rome] decreed that the Jewish people were forbidden to study Torah. Pappus ben Judah saw Rabbi Akiva convening gatherings in public and studying Torah [with them]. Said he to him: "Akiva, are you not afraid of the government?"

Said [Rabbi Akiva] to him: "I'll give you a parable.

"A fox was walking along a river and saw fish rushing to and fro. Said he to them: 'What are you fleeing?'

"Said they to him: 'The nets that the humans spread for us.'

"Said he to them: 'Why don't you come out onto the dry land? We'll live together, as my ancestors lived with your ancestors."

"Said they to him: 'Are you the one of whom it is said that you are the wisest of animals? You're not wise, but foolish! If, in our environment of life we have cause for fear, how much more so in the environment of our death!'

"The same applies to us. If now, when we sit and study the Torah, of which it is said (Deuteronomy 30:20), 'For it is your life and the lengthening of your days,' such is our situation, how much more so if we neglect it. . . ."

Appendix B

PAUL JOHNSON, *A HISTORY OF THE JEWS* (NEW
YORK: HARPER PERENNIAL, 1988), P. 585

Certainly, the world without the Jews would
have been a radically different place. Humanity might have eventually stumbled upon all the
Jewish insights. But we cannot be sure. All the
great conceptual discoveries of the human intel-
lect seem obvious and inescapable once they had
been revealed, but it requires a special genius to
formulate them for the first time. The Jews had
this gift. To them we owe the idea of equality
before the law, both divine and human; of the
sanctity of life and the dignity of a human person;
of the individual conscience and so of a personal
redemption; of the collective conscience and so
of social responsibility; of peace as an abstract
ideal and love as the foundation of justice, and
many other items which constitute the basic
moral furniture of the human mind. Without
Jews it might have been a much emptier place.

PAUL JOHNSON

English journalist, historian,
speechwriter, and author. Johnson
came to prominence in the 1950s as a
journalist writing for, and later editing,
New Statesman, a British political and
cultural magazine. He has written
more than 40 books, many on the
topic of history, and has contributed to
numerous magazines and newspapers.
In 2006, Johnson was honored with
the Presidential Medal of Freedom.

Appendix C

RABBI JONATHAN SACKS, *RADICAL THEN*, *RADICAL NOW* (LONDON: CONTINUUM, 2003), PP. 38–43

At some stage, each of us must decide how to live our lives. We have many options, and no generation in history has had a wider choice. We can live for work or success or fame or power. We can have a whole series of lifestyles and relationships. We can explore any of a myriad of faiths, mysticisms, or therapies. There is only one constraint—namely, that however much of anything else we have, we have only one life, and it is short. How we live and what we live for are the most fateful decisions we ever make. . . .

Imagine that we are in a vast library. In every direction we look there are bookcases. Each has shelves stretching from the floor to the ceiling, and every shelf is full of books. We are surrounded by the recorded thoughts of many people, some great, some less so, and we can reach out and take any book we wish. All we have to do is choose. We begin to read, and for a while we are immersed in the world, real or imaginary, of the writer. It may intrigue us enough to lead us to look for other books by the same writer, or perhaps others on the same subject. Alternatively, we can break off and try a different subject, a different approach; there is no limit. Once the book no longer interests us, we can put it back on the shelf, where it will wait for the next reader to pick it up. It makes no claim on us. It is just a book.

That, for the contemporary secular culture of the West, is what identity is like. We are browsers in

RABBI JONATHAN SACKS, PHD
1948–

Former chief rabbi of the United Kingdom. Rabbi Sacks attended Cambridge University and received his doctorate from King's College, London. A prolific and influential author, his books include *Will We Have Jewish Grandchildren?* and *The Dignity of Difference.* He received the Jerusalem Prize in 1995 for his contributions to enhancing Jewish life in the Diaspora, was knighted and made a life peer in 2005, and became Baron Sacks of Aldridge in 2009.

the library. There are many different ways of living, and none exercises any particular claim on us . . . The various lifestyles into which we enter are like books we read. We are always free to change them, put them back on the shelf. They are what we read, not what we are.

Judaism asks us to envisage an altogether different possibility. Imagine that, while browsing in the library, you come across one book, unlike the rest, which catches your eye because on its spine is written the name of your family. Intrigued, you open it and see many pages written by different hands in different languages. You start reading it, and gradually you start beginning to understand what it is. It is the story each generation of your ancestors has told for the sake of the next, so that everyone born into the family can know where they came from, what happened to them, what they lived for and why. As you turn the pages, you reach the last, which carries no entry but a heading. It bears your name.

According to the intellectual conventions of modernity, this should make no difference. There is nothing in the past that can bind you in the present, no history that can make a difference to who you are and who you are free to be. But this cannot be the whole truth. Were I to find myself holding such a book in my hands, my life would already have been changed. Seeing my name and the story of my forebears, I could not read it as if it were just one story among others . . . Once I knew it existed, I could not put the book back on the shelf and forget about it, because I would now know that I am part of a long line of people who traveled toward a certain destination and whose journey remains unfinished, dependent on me to take it further. . . .

This is more than an imaginative exercise. There is such a book, and to be a Jew is to be a life, a chapter, in it. This book contains the knowledge of who I am and is perhaps the most important thing I can be given.

If Torah Is Divine Wisdom, Why Doesn't It Read That Way?

By Rabbi Tzvi Freeman

Hello Ask-the-Rabbi Rabbi,
I'm kinda disappointed about this Torah. I keep reading on your site about it being the ultimate divine wisdom. To me, it reads like a book of stories.
If it's really a divine document, shouldn't it read more like one of those ancient mystical texts, like the wild and wonderful Zohar or the cryptic and mystical *Book of Formation*?
—Ms. Stick

Hello Ms. Stick,
Now isn't that amazing—the Zohar itself addresses your question:[1]
Rabbi Shimon said:
Woe to the person who thinks that Torah comes simply to tell stories and speak of earthly matters. If that were so, even in our times we could make a Torah, and we could do a much better job of it. If Torah is just to tell of matters of this world, then the famous people of the world today have much better stories to tell. We should chase after them and compose a Torah from them. Rather, all the words of the Torah are sublime matters and deep secrets.
Come and see: There is a higher world and a lower world, and the two are in a single balance. Israel is below, and the angels are way above. Concerning those supernal angels, it is written, "He makes the winds His angels."
That is why, when one of these angels comes below, it must dress itself in the clothing of this world. If it would not do so, it would not be able to enter this world, and the world would not be able to endure it.

If this is so with angels, how much more so with the Torah that creates those angels and creates the entire world—and for which the entire world is sustained. If the Torah would enter this world without being dressed in earthly clothing, the world would not be able to endure.
The stories of the Torah are its clothing. Someone who considers this clothing to be the actual Torah, and imagines that is all there is to the Torah—his spirit expires from him, and he has no portion in the world to come.
That is why David said, "Open my eyes and I will gaze upon the wonders of Your Torah." He wanted to see that which is beneath the clothing of the Torah.
Come and see: Clothing is visible to all. There are fools who see a person dressed in beautiful clothes, and see no further. But clothes are of value only because there is a body within them, and the body is of value only because of its soul. Similarly, the Torah has a body. These are the mitzvahs of the Torah, which are called the body of the Torah, and that body comes clothed in earthly stories.
The fools of the world look at that clothing, those stories of the Torah, and they know no more and look no further to see what is within the clothing. But those who know better don't look at the clothing. They see the body that is within it.
The wise, who are servants of the supernal King, they are those who stand upon Mount Sinai. All they see is the soul, which is the most important of the entire Torah. And there are times when they can see the soul of the soul of the Torah.
Come and see: Above, as well, there is clothing, body, soul, and soul of the soul. The heavens and its host, they are the clothing. The community of Israel, they are the body, and they receive a soul that is the beauty of Israel. This makes them a

---

1.　Zohar III:152a.

body to the soul. This soul of which we speak, which is the beauty of Israel, this is the actual Torah. And the soul of the soul, that is the Holy Ancient One. All of these unite one with the other. Woe to those wicked people who say that the Torah is only a story, and see only that clothing. Fortunate are those good people that see the Torah as it should be seen.

As wine must be contained in a bottle, so the Torah must be contained in this clothing, these stories. But you must look deeper, for all the words and all the stories are no more than clothing.

It comes out that you're right: Taking the Torah as a collection of stories is like talking to a mannequin—the clothes are there, but no one's inside. Might as well read Harry Potter.

But when you probe deeper to uncover the secrets beneath those stories, only then does the Torah begin to shine. It shines a light so intense, so boundless, that the only way it could enter this world is dressed in these simple stories of Jacob and Esau, Joseph and his brothers, Moses and the Children of Israel, and many more.

ANOTHER MYSTERY

But the Zohar is a very mysterious work. Even as it reveals its secrets, it creates yet more mystery. Here, as well, it leaves us with a puzzle to solve:

Many holy books have been written to transmit sublime matters and deep secrets of the universe, of the soul and of the Creator. The Zohar itself is one of them. These books exist in our world. And yet, despite the Zohar's warning, our world continues to exist.

So, back to the same question: If these books can exist in our world without being dressed in earthly matters, why can't the Torah as a whole?

The answer is that the Zohar and other mystical works never truly entered into our world. Not without those simple stories. Yes, the ink lies on physical paper, but their true meaning remains beyond our grasp. They're just not part of our world. They demand that we leave behind our materialistic mindset and enter into a pure

realm of the spirit. Otherwise we're blowing soap bubbles, drawing pictures in the sky.

And the truth is that even those secrets a truly enlightened spirit would gain from the Zohar are still not yet anywhere near the entire depth of the Torah. The Torah is the mind and will of the Creator. How could a created being, no matter how spiritual, possibly see things as its Creator does? An infinite Creator doesn't fit inside any words or ideas. Not even kabbalistic words and ideas.

So the Torah entered the world in a way that it could be grasped by all those who live practical lives down here, even a simple child. And what's its deep-diving suit? Those simple stories.

So that when a small child reads about, say, Jacob and Esau, and grasps the lesson dressed within it, the child grasps that which "creates those angels and creates the entire world—and for which the entire world is sustained." Just because it's dressed up in some clothes doesn't mean there's any less in there. There's a great big Creator of the universe in there.

THE ART GALLERY

Now, let's ask a question: Let's say we are the elite. Let's say we're hyper-spiritual super-holy sages, and we want to learn Torah. Do we skip the stories, since that's just clothing? What about the body of the Torah—the dos and don'ts: do we skip those too and go straight for the soul—meaning, straight to the secrets taught in the writings of the Kabbalah?

So here is a parable that will help to answer that question. It's a parable given by Rabbi Bere Wolf Kozhevnikov, rabbi of Yekatrinoslav at the end of the 19th century.

Imagine you are strolling through an art gallery. You come across three people sitting on a bench before a large painting. Each sits in a different pose—one very enthused, one quite annoyed, and the third in utter stillness, mesmerized. We'll call them Enthused, Annoyed and Mesmerized.

You ask Enthused, "What's so exciting? It's just a painting of a bird in the forest."

Enthused answers, "Just a painting? It's magnificent! See how beautiful the artist made that bird! So realistic! And yet even more beautiful than the real thing!"

So now you turn to Annoyed, and you ask, "What's so annoying? Isn't it a beautiful painting? Look how lovely the bird and the trees!" Annoyed answers, "Beautiful shmutiful. My dear friend, I know the artist personally. The artist is a person of deep spirit, a sage in all ways, with a mind that puts the greatest philosophers of our time to shame. And this is what this sage is renowned for? For a colorful painting of a silly little bird upon a tree?"

Fair enough. Now you turn to Mesmerized. "Excuse me! Ummm, person, hello! HELLO!" Finally, Mesmerized turns and stares at your face, slowly coming back to this world. You say, "Really sorry to disturb you, but, you know, you really shouldn't be so mesmerized with this painting. If you would know the artist, well, he's a great philosopher, a deep thinker, and . . ."

"Yes," Mesmerized interrupts, "I know the artist well. And I am amazed how such a great mind has managed to fit so much brilliance in the details of such a simple scene of a bird upon a tree."

G-D IN THE DETAILS

One of the fathers of modern architecture, Mies van der Rohe, was fond of saying, "G-d is in the details." Every good artist knows this. Take the enigmatic smile of the Mona Lisa, or the rigorous detail-work in the hands and wrinkles of Rembrandt's portraits of the elderly. There's something about simple details and fine subtleties that allow endless beauty to pour through an otherwise run-of-the-mill creation.

Try this: Take some profound idea you've spent much time learning and thinking about. Say, the meaning of life. Or how to achieve happiness. Or "what is love?" Or "what is G-d?" Or even just some new concept you want to market. Now try to explain your thoughts to a five-year-old. Bringing into his language. Use metaphors from his world. Keep to the point, without diluting it, but clarifying it and polishing it until it shines in its simplicity.

If you do the job all the way, I guarantee you will walk away enlightened. You will grasp the depths of your own ideas in a way that you

never before perceived. You won't believe how much that little kid gave you, just by being so darn innocent and simple.

What did the child do for you? The child awakened a whole new depth of intelligence. The intelligence it takes to fit great ideas in small packages. And with that, everything was moved up a notch.

So too, the only mode of expression for the boundless and infinite is in the most simple, concrete, down-to-earth stories. The details, the nuances, they point us to a deeper beauty underlying that simplicity. And as we explore that beauty, we're driven to a yet more magnificent beauty. And it continues ad infinitum. Indeed, as infinite as divine wisdom may be, far deeper is the wisdom to fit infinite wisdom into finite details.

So that, in that simple story, everything is there. G-d Himself is there. And even a small child can grasp Him there. As long as you know that this is only the clothing, and that the Master Artist Himself lies within.

G-D IN HIS WORLD

That's the stories. But, although you didn't ask, my answer would not be complete if I didn't address the pragmatics of Torah.

The practical lessons are a whole new level. They are not just clothing—they're the body of Torah itself. The clothing is not alive—it only brings out the beauty and the wisdom dressed within it. But the body, every cell is alive.

A soul breathes within that body, a pulse of life driving blood and oxygen into the dos and don'ts. And the very essence of the soul is tied up with that body. Because just as a body without a soul is not a living body, so a soul without a body is an aimless, wandering soul without a home, without meaning or purpose.

A mitzvah, a *halachah*, is not just something you do or do not do. Each do or don't is another droplet of the divine, infinite wisdom from beyond the heavens, condensed and crystallized into physical actions performed with physical objects by a physical being—you. Immersed within that action, your entire being becomes a vehicle for that which is too great for infinite multiverses to contain. Through you, unbounded light openly makes its way into this world.

Let me put it this way: Just as you can't build a relationship with a person so long as you consider them no more than a slab of meat, so you can't feel the depth of Torah unless you look deeply into its eyes, ask the right questions, and then drink in with thirst the words of our sages that await those questions.

And yet you can study a person, and understand as much of that person that is possible to understand, and still not have any relationship with that person. Not until you have done something for that person, something that person deeply desires.

So too, and much more so: You can plumb the depths of esoteric wisdom and beat the angels at their own game—and even then, you are only grasping that which is possible for a created being to grasp. Let's not fool ourselves—we are mere fantasies of G-d, a nothingness imagining that it can fathom the mind that conjured it out of nothing. What relationship can there possibly be?

So G-d says to us, "Do this mitzvah, please, for Me."

And now you have all of your Creator—even that which defies understanding. In the act of a mitzvah, the created and the Creator become one.[2]

---

2.   For more on the above, see *Tanya*, chapter 4.

The Gift of an Inheritance and a Heritage

By Yosil Rosenzweig

Every parent would like to leave an inheritance to children and grandchildren; some even work their entire lives, denying themselves vacations and little luxuries, in order to amass some sort of nest-egg as an inheritance. Others live in disappointed frustration because they fear they will not have the wherewithal to leave behind a sizable "will and testimony." What does our Torah have to say about a proper bequest for future generations?

The Torah has two similar words that relate to bequest, Morasha and Yerusha; the first is generally translated as heritage, the second as inheritance. This week's portion of Va'Eira mentions Morasha for the first time:

"And I will bring you into the land concerning which I raised My hand to give it to Abraham, to Isaac, and to Jacob; and I will give it to you for a heritage [Morasha]: I am God" (Exodus 6:8).

It is interesting to note that in Webster's Dictionary the words heritage and inheritance are virtually synonymous. Heritage is defined as "property that is or can be inherited." Biblical Hebrew, however, is very precise and exact; different words have different meanings—there are no synonyms. The different contexts in which the two words Morasha and Yerusha appear can be very revealing about different kind of bequests—and even different kinds of relationships between parents and children, different priorities handed down from generation to generation—which these bequests engender.

We might then explore four different distinctions in meaning between the terms Yerusha and Morasha, inheritance and heritage, which should provide important instruction and inspiration to parents in determining and defining their bequests to their children.

First, the Jerusalem Talmud speaks of Yerusha as something that comes easily. A person dies, leaves an inheritance, and the heir is not required to do anything at all except receive the gift. But just being there is not enough when it comes to Morasha. The Jerusalem Talmud says that the extra letter "Mem" in this word is a grammatical sign of intensity. In order for an individual to come into possession of a Morasha, he has to work for it. An inheritance is what you get from the previous generation, without your particular input; a heritage requires your active involvement and participation. A Yerusha is a check your father left you; a Morasha is a business which your parent may have started, but into which you put much sweat, blood and tears, your own efforts and energies.

In order to further emphasize this point, the Torah generally uses the term Morasha (heritage) only in reference to Torah and the Land of Israel. When the Twelve Tribes of Israel are blessed at the end of Devarim (Deuteronomy), the Torah declares:

"Moses prescribed the Torah to us, an eternal heritage (Morasha) for the congregation of Jacob"—Devarim 33:4.

Furthermore, the Babylonian Talmud says there are three gifts which G-d gave the Jewish people that can only be acquired through commitment and suffering: "Torah, the Land of Israel and the World to Come" (Berachot 5a). We understand that neither Torah, the Land of Israel, nor the World to Come is acquired passively. The Talmudic sages specifically teach that "Torah is not a Yerusha (an inheritance)," which comes automatically to a child. All achievement in Torah depends on an individual's own efforts and desire. Maimonides states:

"...on the path of Torah acquisition...no one can merit the crown of Torah unless he is willing to destroy his desire for materialism while in pursuit of Torah expertise."

Similarly, the Land of Israel cannot be acquired without "sacrifice and suffering," and those two words take on different meanings as we pass through history. Nothing is more apparent in modern Israel today. A heritage comes hard, not easy, and our national heritage is Torah and Israel. And of course the World to Come can only be acquired by a life of dedication to HaShem's will.

The second difference between Morasha and Yerusha is bound up with the first. The sages of the Midrash tie the word Morasha to a cognate term which sounds similar; *do not only read Morasha but also read M'orasah, fiancée, or my betrothed.* The kind of emotion one feels for a fiancée is precisely that which provides an individual with strength, courage and commitment to work tirelessly and to willingly sacrifice. Yerusha requires no special feeling. Morasha, however, demands emotional commitment. And so it has always been regarding Torah, Israel and the World of Come, for our Jewish people.

Torah is not just another intellectual pursuit. Does the chairman of the philosophy department walk through the library stacks, kissing copies of Aristotle if they fall to the floor, or dance with the collected writings of Plato? But we kiss the Torah whenever it is taken from the ark, and we have a special holiday dedicated to dancing with the Torah. And when we learn Torah, it is often with a melody, the expressions of the heart.

Third, the difference between Yerusha and Morasha is the difference between that which is tangible and that which is intangible. You can put your hands on a Yerusha; you can put it in the bank or hang it on the wall. A Morasha, however, does not have to be so. You need not touch it in order to feel it. It can be an idea, an ideal—a way of life.

A Yiddish poem puts it very well:

> "My parents couldn't leave me a car, but they left me a prayer: 'Go with G-d.'
> My parents couldn't leave me money, but they left me a charge: 'Give to those less fortunate.'
> My parents couldn't leave me jewelry, but they left me an ideal: 'Be a Mensch.'
> All I got was words. They only left me words, but those words are the bedrock of my life."

The last distinction is probably the most important. A Yerusha is something which can be depleted, wasted. Even the largest amount of money bequeathed can be squandered, or legitimately lost. In contrast, a Morasha must be given over intact to the next generation. Its grammatical form means "to hand over to someone else." Silver is an inheritance, and can be spent, melted down or used in whatever way the inheritor desires. But a pair of silver candlesticks is a heritage, an heirloom meant to be passed down and used from parent to child. Tragically, many of us focus too much on inheritance and too little on heritage. We pass down money and material goods, but not meaning and a message. We pass down items but not ideals; possessions but not principles. Jewish parents have bequeathed the ideals of Torah and Israel to their children for 3,300 years, and that's the secret behind our continued vitality to this very day.

Never mind your inheritance. The real question is: What will be the heritage that you will bequeath to your children? I have a very close friend who recently bewailed the fact that she wasn't given the tools to appreciate her heritage from her parents. Only recently through contact with Torah personalities was she able to appreciate her Judaism. Perhaps in dealing with the Jewish continuity debate and discussion, we need to consider our use of language. What, in fact, are we continuing?

It is not a matter of inheritance as much as heritage. It is this sense of "Morasha" that endures and inspires our successors in subsequent generations. The most valuable inheritance, then, is a sense of heritage.

We need then to more effectively communicate a sense of intimacy and warmth with the message of our faith and with the lessons of our personal and collective histories; for this is the legacy that lasts, the gift that survives beyond our physical journey.

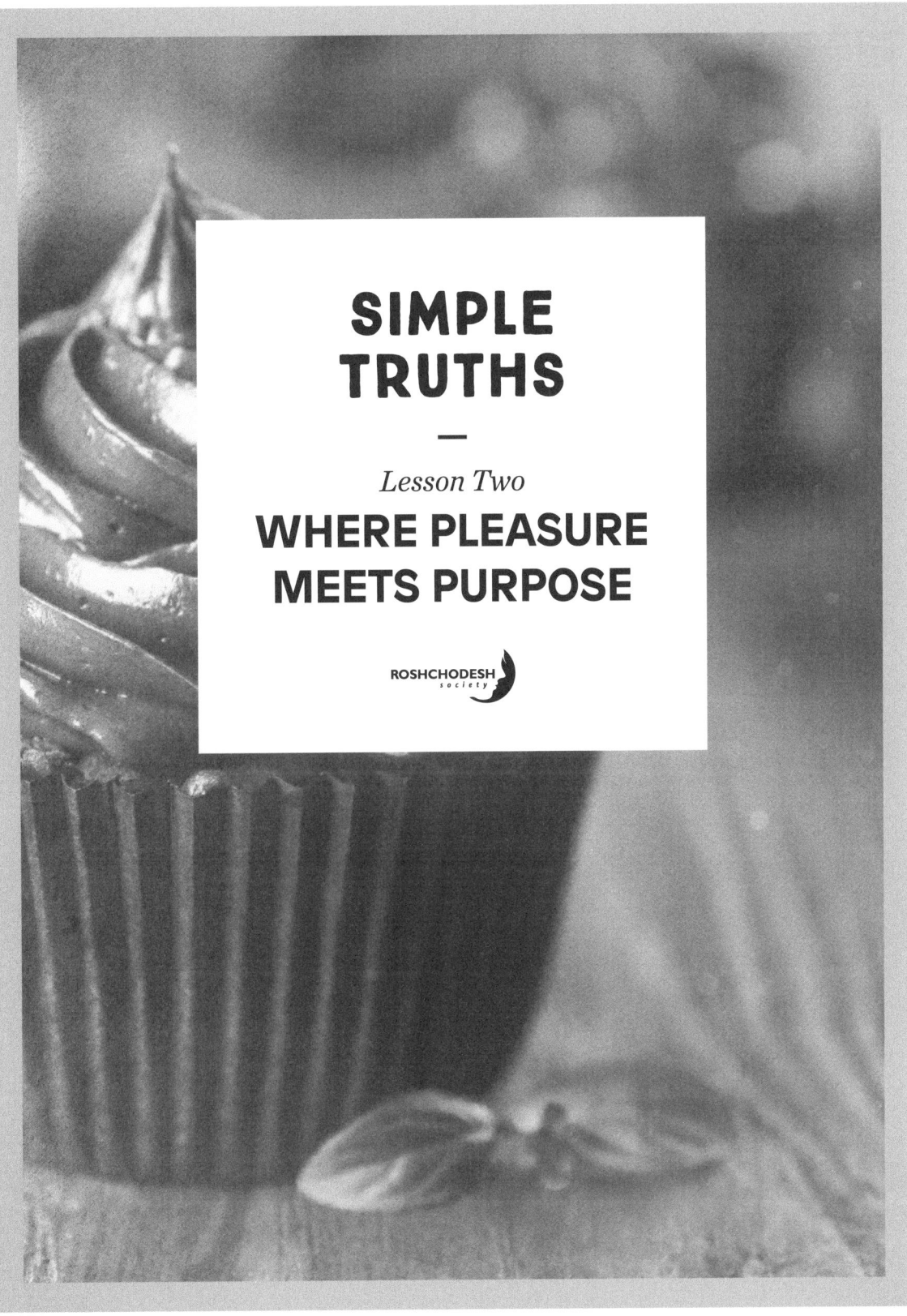

SIMPLE TRUTHS

—

Lesson Two

WHERE PLEASURE MEETS PURPOSE

ROSHCHODESH
society

THE PRIMARY HUMAN DRIVE—
PLEASURE VS. PURPOSE

Exercise 1

On a scale from 1 to 4, how important is pleasure to living a good life?

On a scale from 1 to 4, how important is purpose to living a good life?

_____

1) Very important, 2) Important, 3) Not so important, 4) Not important at all

Question for Discussion

Do you agree or disagree with the pleasure principle as the most instinctual driver of human behavior?

Text 1

DAVID J. LINDEN, "THE NEUROSCIENCE OF PLEASURE,"
WWW.HUFFINGTONPOST.COM, JULY 7, 2011

In the 1930s, the psychologist B. F. Skinner devised the operant conditioning chamber, or "Skinner box," in which a lever pressed by an animal triggered either a reinforcing stimulus, such as delivery of food or water, or a punishing stimulus, such as a painful foot shock. Rats placed in a Skinner box will rapidly learn to press a lever for a food reward and to avoid pressing a lever that delivers the shock.

In the 1950s, the psychologists James Olds and Peter Milner modified the chamber so that a lever press would deliver direct brain stimulation through deep implanted electrodes. What resulted was perhaps the most dramatic experiment in the history of behavioral neuroscience: Rats would press the lever as many as 7,000 times per hour to stimulate their brains. This was a pleasure center, a reward circuit, the activation of which was much more powerful than any natural stimulus.

DAVID J. LINDEN, PHD
1961—

A professor in the Solomon H. Snyder Department of Neuroscience at the Johns Hopkins University School of Medicine, his laboratory has worked for many years on the cellular substrates of memory storage, recovery of function following brain injury, and a few other topics. He served for many years as the chief editor of the *Journal of Neurophysiology*.

A series of subsequent experiments revealed that rats preferred pleasure circuit stimulation to food (even when they were hungry) and water (even when they were thirsty). Self-stimulating male rats would ignore a female in heat and would repeatedly cross foot-shock-delivering floor grids to reach the lever. Female rats would abandon their newborn nursing pups to continually press the lever. Some rats would self-stimulate as often as 2,000 times per hour for 24 hours, to the exclusion of all other activities. They had to be unhooked from the apparatus to prevent death by self-starvation. Pressing that lever became their entire world.

Questions for Discussion

1. If you could be hooked up to a machine that would stimulate your brain's pleasure center at the press of a button, would you do it?

2. If you could stay hooked up to such a machine for a year of your life, would you do it?

Text 2

IBID.

Patient B-19, a 24-year-old male . . . of average intelligence who suffered from depression and obsessive-compulsive tendencies, was wheeled into the operating room. Electrodes were implanted at nine different sites in deep regions of his brain. . . . When Patient B-19 was finally allowed free access to the [pleasure] stimulator, he quickly began mashing the button like an 8-year-old playing Donkey Kong. According to the paper, "During these sessions, B-19 stimulated himself to a point that, both behaviorally and introspectively, he was experiencing an almost overwhelming euphoria and elation and had to be disconnected despite his vigorous protests."

Lest anyone think that it is only men—creatures of inherently base urges—who would respond in this manner, another recorded case, performed by a different group, involved a woman who received an electrode implant in her thalamus, an adjacent deep brain structure, to control chronic pain. This technique has proven effective for some patients whose severe pain is not well-controlled by drugs. However, in this patient the stimulation spread to nearby brain structures, producing an intense [pleasure]: "At its most frequent, the patient self-stimulated throughout the day, neglecting her personal hygiene and family commitments. A chronic ulceration developed at the tip of the finger used to adjust the amplitude dial and she frequently tampered with the device in an effort to increase the stimulation amplitude. At times she implored her family to limit her access to the stimulator, each time demanding its return after a short hiatus."

Text 3

VIKTOR FRANKL, *MAN'S SEARCH FOR MEANING*
(BOSTON, MA: BEACON PRESS, 2006), P. 101

A man who becomes conscious of the responsibility he bears toward a human being who affectionately waits for him, or to an unfinished work, will never be able to throw away his life. He who knows the "why" for his existence, will be able to bear almost any "how."

VIKTOR EMIL FRANKL
1905–1997

MD, PhD, founder of logotherapy. Frankl was professor of neurology and psychiatry at the University of Vienna Medical School. During World War II, he spent three years in various concentration camps, including Theresienstadt, Auschwitz, and Dachau. Frankl was founder of the psychotherapeutic school called logotherapy. Frankl authored 39 books, which have been published in 38 languages. His most famous book, *Man's Search for Meaning*, has sold more than 9 million copies in the U.S. alone.

Questions for Discussion

1. Why were meaning and purpose so important for the mental health of Frankl's patients?

2. Why did these characteristics need to be specifically "selfless?"

TWO SPIRITS, TWO DRIVES

Text 4a

ECCLESIASTES 3:19–21

כְּמוֹת זֶה כֵּן מוֹת זֶה, וְרוּחַ אֶחָד לַכֹּל, וּמוֹתַר הָאָדָם מִן הַבְּהֵמָה אָיִן, כִּי הַכֹּל הָבֶל.

הַכֹּל הוֹלֵךְ אֶל מָקוֹם אֶחָד. הַכֹּל הָיָה מִן הֶעָפָר וְהַכֹּל שָׁב אֶל הֶעָפָר.

מִי יוֹדֵעַ, רוּחַ בְּנֵי הָאָדָם הָעֹלָה הִיא לְמָעְלָה, וְרוּחַ הַבְּהֵמָה הַיֹּרֶדֶת הִיא לְמַטָּה לָאָרֶץ?

As the death of man, so is the death of an animal; each has a vivifying spirit, and the superiority of man over beast is naught, for all is vanity.

All go to one place. All came from the dust, and all return to the dust.

How many understand, however, that the spirit of man ascends on high, while the spirit of the beast descends to the earth?

Text 4b

RABBI SHMUEL ELIEZER EIDEL'S, *CHIDUSHEI AGADOT*, SOTAH 34B

שֶׁיֵּשׁ בָּאָדָם ב׳ רוחות, כְּמוֹ שֶׁכָּתוּב "מִי יוֹדֵעַ רוּחַ הַבְּהֵמָה הַיּוֹרֶדֶת לְמַטָּה, וְרוּחַ הָאָדָם הָעוֹלָה לְמַעְלָה", דְּכוּלָּה בָּאָדָם אַיְירִי, כְּדִבְרֵי הַמְּפָרְשִׁים: רוּחַ הַחִיּוּנִי שֶׁבָּאָדָם שֶׁהוּא מִשְׁתַּוֶוה בּוֹ לִבְהֵמָה, וְרוּחַ הָאַחֶרֶת שֶׁהָאָדָם מוּבְדָּל בּוֹ מִן הַבְּהֵמָה, דְּהַיְינוּ הַנְּשָׁמָה.

There are two spirits within a person, as it is stated, "The spirit of the beast descends to the earth, while the spirit of man ascends on high." The commentaries explain that both refer to the human. There is the "spirit of the animal" [within the human], in which man and beast are alike, and there is the spirit by which man is distinct from animal; this is the human soul.

RABBI SHMUEL ELIEZER HALEVI EIDEL'S (MAHARSHA)
1555–1632

Rabbi, author, and Talmudist. Rabbi Eidel's established a yeshivah in Posen, Poland, which was supported by his mother-in-law, Eidel (hence his surname is "Eidel's"). He is primarily known for his *Chidushei Halachot,* a commentary on the Talmud in which he resolves difficulties in the texts of the Talmud, Rashi, and *Tosafot,* and which is a basic work for those who seek an in-depth understanding of the Talmud; and for his *Chidushei Agadot,* his innovative commentary on the homiletic passages of the Talmud.

Questions for Discussion

Are our drives for pleasure (which stem from the human soul) and purpose (which stem from the Godly soul) mutually exclusive? Must they always contradict one another?

SHEMA YISRAEL—GOD IS ONE
ONE VS. ONLY

Text 5

DEUTERONOMY 6:4

שְׁמַע יִשְׂרָאֵל, ה׳ אֱלֹקֵינוּ, ה׳ אֶחָד.

Hear, O Israel: The Lord is our God; the Lord is one.

Question for Discussion

What is the message of the Shema?

Text 6

RABBI YOSEF KARO, *SHULCHAN ARUCH, ORACH CHAYIM* 61:6

צָרִיךְ לְהַאֲרִיךְ בְּחֵי״ת שֶׁל אֶחָד, כְּדֵי שֶׁיַּמְלִיךְ הַקָּדוֹשׁ בָּרוּךְ
הוּא בַּשָּׁמַיִם וּבָאָרֶץ . . . וְיַאֲרִיךְ בְּדָלֵי״ת שֶׁל אֶחָד שִׁעוּר
שֶׁיַּחֲשׁוֹב שֶׁהַקָּדוֹשׁ בָּרוּךְ הוּא יָחִיד בְּעוֹלָמוֹ וּמוֹשֵׁל בְּד׳ רוּחוֹת
הָעוֹלָם . . .

וְיֵשׁ נוֹהֲגִים לְהַטּוֹת הָרֹאשׁ כְּפִי הַמַּחֲשָׁבָה: מַעֲלָה וּמַטָּה וּלְד׳
רוּחוֹת.

One has to take one's time when saying the *chet* [whose numerical value is eight] of *echad*, enough time to mentally crown God as King over the [seven] heavens and the earth. . . . One should then lengthen the saying of the *dalet* [whose numerical value is four] of *echad,* sufficient time to consider how God is the only One in His universe and how He rules over all [that is in] the four directions of the world. . . .

There are those whose custom it is to slightly incline their heads according to their thoughts— upward, downward, and to the four directions.

RABBI YOSEF CARO (MARAN, *BEIT YOSEF*)
1488–1575

Halachic authority and author. Rabbi Caro was born in Spain, but was forced to flee during the expulsion in 1492 and eventually settled in Safed, Israel. He authored many works including the *Beit Yosef, Kesef Mishneh,* and a mystical work, *Magid Meisharim.* Rabbi Caro's magnum opus, the Shulchan Aruch (Code of Jewish Law), has been universally accepted as the basis for modern Jewish law.

Text 7

RABBI YANKI TAUBER, "THE NUMEROLOGY OF REDEMPTION," (BASED ON THE TEACHINGS OF THE LUBAVITCHER REBBE), CHABAD.ORG/2741

It was to express *echad*-ness that He created the world, created man, granted him freedom of choice, and commanded him the Torah. He created existences that, at least in their own perception, are distinct of Him, and gave them the tools to bring their lives into utter harmony with His will. When a diverse and plural world chooses, by its own initiative, to unite with Him, the divine oneness assumes a new, deeper expression: G-d is *echad*.

RABBI YANKI TAUBER

1965–

Chasidic scholar and author. A native of Brooklyn, NY, Rabbi Tauber is an internationally renowned author who specializes in adapting the teachings of the Lubavitcher Rebbe. He is a member of the JLI curriculum development team, and has written numerous articles and books, including *Once Upon a Chassid* and *Beyond the Letter of the Law*.

THE MASK

Text 8

RABBI SHNE'UR ZALMAN OF LIADI, *TORAH OR*, *VA'ERA* 57A

וְלָכַךְ נִקְרָאִים בְּשֵׁם קְלִיפוֹת, שֶׁהֵם כְּמָשָׁל הַקְּלִיפָה שֶׁהִיא חוֹפֶפֶת וּמַקֶּפֶת עַל הַפְּרִי הַכָּנוּס בְּתוֹכָהּ וּמַסְתֶּרֶת אוֹתָהּ, כְּמָשָׁל קְלִיפַּת הָאֱגוֹז. וְאֵין תְּרוּפָה לְהוֹצִיא הַפְּרִי כִּי אִם עַל יְדֵי שְׁבִירַת הַקְּלִיפָה.

וְכָךְ, כְּדֵי לְהוֹצִיא נִצוֹצֵי הַקְּדוֹשָׁה מֵהַקְּלִיפוֹת הַמַסְתִּירִים עֲלֵיהֶם, הָיָה צָרִיךְ לִהְיוֹת שְׁבִירַת הַקְּלִיפוֹת.

RABBI SHNE'UR ZALMAN OF LIADI (ALTER REBBE)

1745–1812

Chasidic rebbe, halachic authority, and founder of the Chabad movement. The Alter Rebbe was born in Liozna, Belarus, and was among the principal students of the Magid of Mezeritch. His numerous works include the *Tanya*, an early classic containing the fundamentals of Chabad Chasidism, and *Shulchan Aruch HaRav*, an expanded and reworked code of Jewish law.

Therefore the [spiritual forces that God created to counteract His holiness] are referred to [in the mystical works] as *kelipot* (husks). *Kelipah* can be compared to the husk that encompasses, surrounds, and conceals from view the fruit stored inside it (e.g., the shell of a walnut). The only way to extract the fruit is to break the husk.

Likewise, the *kelipot* need to be broken to extract the hidden sparks of holiness from their grips.

HARMONY: FUSING PLEASURE WITH PURPOSE

Figure 2.1

Three Categories of Holiness

Holy

Its true purpose, its innate holiness, is obvious and self-understood (no shell/*kelipah*).

Not holy, with the potential to become holy

Its true purpose can be revealed and implemented. It wears a translucent shell that can be removed, allowing its purpose and holiness to shine.

Not holy, with no potential to become holy

Its true purpose cannot be revealed or implemented. It wears a thick, opaque, irremovable shell.

Exercise 2

	Examples	Typical prevalence in daily life
Holy		
Not holy, with potential to become holy		
Not holy, with no potential to become holy		

Question for Discussion

Identify something in your life that you take plea-sure in. How can you rip off its "shell" to reveal its true, holy purpose?

Text 9

RABBI SHNE'UR ZALMAN OF LIADI, *TANYA*, CH. 7

כְּגוֹן דֶּרֶךְ מָשָׁל, הָאוֹכֵל בְּשָׂרָא שְׁמֵינָא דְּתוֹרָא וְשׁוֹתֶה יַיִן
מְבוּשָׂם לְהַרְחִיב דַּעְתּוֹ לַה' וּלְתוֹרָתוֹ, כִּדְאָמַר רָבָא, "חַמְרָא
וְרֵיחָא כוּ'". אוֹ בִּשְׁבִיל כְּדֵי לְקַיֵּים מִצְוַת עֹנֶג שַׁבָּת וְיוֹם טוֹב.
אֲזַי נִתְבָּרֵר חַיּוּת הַבָּשָׂר וְהַיַּיִן שֶׁהָיָה נִשְׁפָּע מִקְּלִיפַּת נוֹגַהּ,
וְעוֹלֶה לַה' כְּעוֹלָה וּכְקָרְבָּן.
וְכֵן הָאוֹמֵר מִילְתָא דִּבְדִיחוּתָא, לְפַקֵּחַ דַּעְתּוֹ וּלְשַׂמֵּחַ לִבּוֹ לַה'
וּלְתוֹרָתוֹ וַעֲבוֹדָתוֹ שֶׁצְּרִיכִים לִהְיוֹת בְּשִׂמְחָה, וּכְמוֹ שֶׁעָשָׂה
רָבָא לְתַלְמִידָיו שֶׁאָמַר לִפְנֵיהֶם מִילְתָא דִּבְדִיחוּתָא תְּחִלָּה
וּבַדְחֵי רַבָּנָן.

For instance, say one eats a prime cut of beef and drinks flavorful wine in order to expand his mind to better serve God and [study] His Torah (as [the Talmudic sage] Rava said, "Wine and [a pleasant] fragrance [make my mind more receptive]" [Yoma 76a]), or in order to fulfill the commandment to enjoy the Shabbat and the festivals. [In this instance,] the divine spark within the meat and the wine is extracted from the clutches of the [redeemable form of] *kelipah* and ascends to God like a burnt offering and a sacrifice.

The same is true regarding one who makes a humorous remark to sharpen his mind and make his heart rejoice in God and His Torah and His service, which should be practiced joyfully. Indeed, Rava was wont to do this with his pupils: he would preface his discourses with a humorous remark, whereupon the students would laugh [and the lightened mood made them more receptive and better able to understand the discourse].

Exercise 3

1. Think of your favorite food. Think of how you can use the energy and expansive mood that you gain after partaking of that food in order to serve God.

2. Think of a talent or passion you have. Think of a way you can use it to better the world, e.g., to bring joy to those around you, or to serve God

UNITING THE FRAGMENTS

Text 10
DEUTERONOMY 6:9

וּכְתַבְתָּם עַל מְזֻזוֹת בֵּיתֶךָ וּבִשְׁעָרֶיךָ.

And you shall inscribe them upon the doorposts
of your house and upon your gates.

My Personal Take

In the space provided below, write down, in your
own words, the simple truth you learned in today's lesson.

שְׁמַע יִשְׂרָאֵל ה׳ Hear O Israel, the Lord is
אֱלֹקֵינוּ ה׳ אֶחָד. our God, God is One.

Key Points

1. In the Jewish view, the natural human drives for pleasure and purpose are not mutually exclusive, but compatible; our pleasure must be purposeful—and our purpose, pleasurable.

2. The Jewish concept of monotheism means not just that there is one God, but that God is *one*—the idea of divine unity. Everything is an expression and manifestation of God, and all of existence is in harmony with the divine plan.

3. The challenge in perceiving God's oneness comes from the fact that the world wears a "shell" or *kelipah* that conceals the truth of God's existence. The *Shema* charges us to look deeper and find and reveal the unifying force within the multiplicity.

4. The unique role of Jews is to live our lives in a way that reveals God's oneness in the world. We do that by infusing every part of our lives, including and especially, the pleasures and luxuries we enjoy, with a higher purpose. In doing so, we reveal that God is *one*—that He permeates all of reality.

5. All of the activities and parts of our lives—despite feeling disconnected from one another and from a higher purpose—are unified by the mission of *Shema*—to reveal Godliness in the world. This, perhaps, is a deeper reason that we affix a mezuzah to every doorpost of our homes.

Laws of Reciting the Shema

By Rabbi Aryeh Citron

Chapter six of Deuteronomy (verses 4–9) contains the first paragraph of the Shema. In verse 7 we read: "And you shall teach them to your sons and speak of them—when you sit in your house, and when you walk on the way, and when you lie down and when you rise up." Our Sages explained that the words "when you lie down and when you rise up" is a charge to recite the Shema every morning and evening. The Shema includes three paragraphs. The theme of the first (Deuteronomy 6:4–9) is the acceptance of the "yoke of Heaven"; of the second (ibid., 11:13–21), the acceptance of the yoke of His commandments; and of the third (Numbers 15:37–41), remembering the Exodus from Egypt.

Our sages tell us that the creation of the entire world is considered a worthwhile endeavor just for the acceptance of the yoke of Heaven that we enact during the daily recital of Shema. It is said that one who prepares himself for prayer in the proper way, puts on *tefillin*, recites the Shema, and then prays, has fully accepted the yoke of Heaven.

The *Sefer HaChinuch* writes that when a person reciting Shema remembers the unity and kingship of the Almighty, who supervises everything, he will take to heart that G-d's eyes observe all of a person's ways. He will appreciate that G-d counts our steps, and that none of our thoughts are hidden from Him. Thinking this and saying this will guard a person throughout the day. Repeating it at night will guard him at night as well.

The reward for reciting the Shema at the right time is greater than the reward for studying Torah during the rest of the day, and Torah study is considered greater than all the other mitzvot.

WHO IS OBLIGATED TO READ THE SHEMA?

As the recitation of the Shema is a "time-bound" positive mitzvah, women are not obligated to read the Shema at a particular time. Nevertheless, it is proper that they recite at least the first verse in order to accept upon themselves the yoke of Heaven. In addition, they should recite the blessing after the Shema, in order to remember the Exodus from Egypt. Children who have reached the "age of *chinuch* (education)," i.e., who are capable of reciting the Shema, should be trained to read the Shema on time.

BLESSINGS OF THE SHEMA

Our sages instituted blessings that should be recited before and after the morning and evening Shema. These are called the Birchot Keriat Shema ("blessings of the Shema recital").

1. These blessings should be recited as part of the daily morning and evening prayer services, so that they are followed immediately by the Amidah.
2. If one is praying these prayers within the proper time slot for reciting the Shema (see below), he will automatically fulfill the mitzvah of reciting the Shema when he recites it within the prayers.
3. If one is praying either of these prayers before or after the proper time for reciting Shema, he should make sure to also recite the Shema within the proper time slot. Nevertheless, he should still say the Shema as part of the prayer.

WHEN TO RECITE THE MORNING SHEMA

1. The best time to recite the morning Shema is after it begins to get light (*"misheyakir"*) but before sunrise. For this reason, many people (people who do so are called *vatikin*) begin praying shortly before sunrise, so that they conclude the Shema and start the Amidah as the sun rises (which is the earliest time to recite the Amidah).
2. One should try to recite Shema as early as possible. It is best to recite the Shema while wearing *tzitzit* and *tefillin*, and as part of the morning prayers. One should therefore try

to pray with the earliest *minyan* that one is able to attend.

3. If one will not pray until later, it is good to say the three paragraphs of Shema as soon as one awakens, after saying the morning blessings. This is especially true for someone who wishes to drink tea or coffee.

4. One may perform the mitzvah of reciting the Shema until the end of the third halachic hour of the day. This means until one quarter of the sunlight hours, counting from sunrise till sunset, have passed. (Some opine that the day's halachic hours start at dawn and end with nightfall.)

5. If one missed that time, he is no longer able to fulfill the mitzvah of reciting the Shema. He should still recite the Shema as part of his morning prayers, but he only receives reward as one who reads verses from the Torah.

THE TIME FOR RECITING THE EVENING SHEMA

The time for reciting the evening Shema begins when three stars become visible in the night sky (this is called *tzeit ha-kochavim*.)

One must recite the Shema before midnight, and one who delays reading it past midnight is called *"over al divrei chachamim"* (one who transgresses the words of the sages). Our sages instituted that one should recite the Shema before midnight, in order to distance oneself from sinning (i.e., forgetting to recite the Shema entirely). Nevertheless, if one reads it afterwards, up until dawn, he has fulfilled his obligation.

If, for reasons beyond one's control (such as illness), one did not say the nighttime Shema before dawn, he may still say it until sunrise.

THE BEDTIME SHEMA

One other time that we say the Shema each day is before going to bed. It is recited as a protection, and so that we go to sleep with words of Torah on our lips. Though it's not part of the mitzvah of reciting the Shema, if one did not yet recite the evening Shema, one can fulfill the mitzvah when reading the bedtime Shema, if that is his intention.

KAVANAH (CONCENTRATION)

1. When one recites the Shema, he should do so tremulously, with concentration, reverence and awe, as people are wont to do when reading a new communication issued by the king. The message of Shema should always be considered precious, like a new message each day, not like an old message that has become stale.

2. Before beginning to read the Shema, one should take a moment to contemplate that he is now going to fulfill G-d's commandment. In addition, one must concentrate on the meaning of Shema's words, at the very least while reciting the verse of Shema. If one did not concentrate on the meaning of the words of this verse, he must repeat it. (If one therefore says the verse twice in a row, he should say it quietly the second time.)

3. Although one should continue concentrating on the meaning of the words for the rest of Shema, if one didn't do so, he has still fulfilled the mitzvah.

4. It is important to have in mind the meanings of the names of G-d employed in the verse of Shema. The Tetragrammaton (pronounced *"Adonai"*) implies that G-d was, is, and will always be—at once (i.e., He is beyond time), and that He is the Master of all. The name *Elohim* (or *Eloheinu*) alludes to His strength and power, and that He has the ability to carry out His will in the upper and lower worlds.

5. Every Hebrew letter also has a numerical value. When saying *echad* ("one"), a person should concentrate on the fact that G-d is the only One (*alef*) in the seven heavens and in the earth (together these equal *chet*, eight) as well as in all four directions (*dalet*). These three letters spell *echad*.

6. "Whoever lengthens the word *echad* is rewarded with a long life." This refers to one who spends time on the aforementioned meditation.

7. When one says the verse of *Ve'ohavtah* ("and you shall love G-d"), he should try to actually introduce love of G-d into his heart.

8. In order to enhance concentration, one may not do anything or even motion to others while reciting the first section of Shema.

While reciting the second and third sections, one may motion to another if it is for the purpose of a mitzvah. For this reason, one should not recite the Shema while driving.

HOW TO RECITE THE SHEMA

1. One may recite the Shema while sitting or standing. Some permit reciting the Shema while laying on one's side. Others only permit this in cases of need. One should not go out of his way to stand for the Shema as our Sages did not require this.

2. One who is walking should stop walking while reciting the first verse and *Baruch Shem* and may then continue walking while reciting the remainder.

3. One should cover his eyes with his right hand while saying the verse of Shema in order to reduce distractions and enhance concentration. For the same reason, the first verse should be said aloud.

4. One should say the first verse as follows: *Shema Yisrael* (Hear, O Israel), pause, *Adonai Eloheinu* (the L-rd is our G-d), pause, *Adonai echad* (the L-rd is one). The pauses emphasize the meaning of the words.

5. The second verse ("*Baruch shem . . .*") is recited in an undertone, except on Yom Kippur when it is recited out loud.

6. One should be careful to enunciate each word and letter of the Shema properly.

7. When saying the morning Shema, men should hold their *tzitzit* and kiss them at certain intervals. See the instructions in the prayer book for more information.

8. If one is praying with a *minyan*, at the end of Shema, one should listen to the cantor repeat the last three words ("*Adonai Eloheichem emet*").

   Our sages tell us that the 248 words of the Shema correspond to the 248 limbs in the (male) body. Each limb is healed by one of the words of Shema. Since the Shema actually only contains 245 words, the *chazzan* repeats the last three words in order to reach the total number of 248. The congregation should listen to these words, even if they have not yet finished reciting the Shema, but they do not repeat them themselves.

   If someone is saying the Shema without a *minyan*, Chabad custom is for the individual to repeat the words "*ani Adonai Eloheichem*" twice.

WHEN IN DOUBT

If one is not sure whether or not he recited the Shema, he must recite it again.

Revealing the Whole in the Parts

By Shana Guzick

When I was a teenager, I used to take art lessons once a week at a private studio. I'd only complete a few pieces in a given year; a couple hours once a week wasn't very much time to finish anything. One of my projects was a ceramic plate. Over a few weeks, I carefully formed it from clay--freely, with my hands, and I fashioned a delicate hamsa (figure of a hand that appears as a common motif in Middle Eastern art) out of softer clay on the plate's surface. After it hardened in the kiln and cooled off over a period of several days, I painted each element with different colors of glaze, making sure the colors went well with each other, wiping away the paint and redoing it over and over until it was perfect.

I had to wait a couple of weeks to get my piece fired the second time to turn the paint glaze into a glossy finish. The week it was supposed to be ready to take home, I arrived excited to class, ready to see my final product. I sat in my seat, waiting impatiently. I watched as the other people in the class got their pieces back, and my neck became tired from turning my head towards the firing room so many times. Finally, my teacher brought out what looked like my plate. Smiling, proud, she approached my workspace. Just before she reached the table, she lost her balance and, in slow motion, I watched the masterpiece I never got to unveil crash to the cold, hard tile, so unyielding and unforgiving.

Cringing, I looked at the floor, now covered in pieces of what used to be my plate. I tried not to show my disappointment to my teacher, who already felt terrible for her mistake. Forcing a smile and holding back tears, I assured her I'd figure out something to do with the pieces. I picked a shard up off the floor. What was it? Could it be a fingertip? Or maybe a piece of a palm? One of the abstract designs in the background? I couldn't make it out. One piece alone might as well have been nothing. I was defeated.

I started to collect the rest of the pieces from the floor to throw away. I placed them all on the table ready to push them into the open, hungry, taunting garbage can. As the first of the pieces hit the bowels of the can with a resounding thud, I noticed that a thin blue line on one of the pieces seemed to flow into a thin blue line on the piece next to it. I picked one piece up with one hand, the next with the other. I held my hands up and brought the two pieces together. Though barely separated by a thin, jagged shadow where they'd been broken apart, they were a perfect fit.

I had made up my mind. I grabbed the discarded pieces out of the garbage can, and I began to reconstruct my new puzzle, gluing piece by piece. By the end of the class, I had a new masterpiece. A well-loved, painfully delicate, perfectly imperfect masterpiece. It wasn't a mistake anymore. It was art. It was whole. Most of us tend to miss the forest for the trees. What we observe, we see as isolated and disconnected. Instead of hearing a song in the noise around us, we hear a series of clangs and screams and vibrations. Instead of seeing a dance, we see a kick, a turn of the head, and a raised arm. The thing is, a kick is just a kick, and a clang is just a clang. A hand doesn't do much good if there's no arm to extend it, and the arm is useless if there are no legs to walk it. Nothing in this world can function on its own. Alone, every single thing in existence is nothing. And yet, if any one morsel of this universe were missing, our world, too, would be nothing. Everything, be it a ceramic shard, a bang on a drum, the palm of a hand, or a human being, is one part of a whole. Sometimes, it takes first being broken to realize what the whole entity is. For the hamsa plate to become complete, it had to first crack into pieces. It hurts when you scrape your knee; suddenly, you're missing a part of it. The heart aches and yearns for years before you find the other half of your soul, which you previously thought to be its own entity.

This is the way of the One who created us not only in His image, but with a spark of Him within us. He created a world in which everything seems discombobulated and solitary deliberately so that we can be the ones to reveal the oneness in it all. He breaks us so that we can glue ourselves back together. Our seemingly unfinished world exists for the sole (and soul) purpose that we should reveal the G-dliness in us by becoming creators ourselves, unveiling the hidden connections between every atom in Creation.

Atonement, too, is about revealing Oneness. The ultimate atonement is to recreate ourselves as beings conscious of the fact that we are all one with each other and with G-d, conscious that we are simultaneously nothing and everything.

May we be blessed with help from Above, that we should all be able to rectify ourselves and be the ones to reveal that we are all broken shards of the same masterpiece.

The Hidden Beauty of the Shema

By Lisa Aiken, PhD

CENTRALITY OF THE SHEMA

Jews say two especially important prayers every day: the Shema and the Amidah. We fulfill the biblical commandment (mitzvah) to say the Shema every morning and evening when we say its first verse, "Hear, Israel, the Lord is our God, the Lord is One." The rabbis, however, required us to add three additional paragraphs, drawn from the books of Deuteronomy and Numbers. Besides our reciting the Shema daily, we also say it before going to sleep, over a baby boy the night before his ritual circumcision (brit milah), and before we die.

The commandments to which the Shema refers—tefillin (leather boxes containing parchments that are put on a man's head and arm), mezuzah (a parchment with Torah verses that we put on our doorposts), Tzitzit (fringes that are put on a four-cornered garment), and remembering the Exodus from Egypt—are also part of our daily lives.

Thus, the Shema literally accompanies us from cradle to grave. The Minchat Chinuch explains why the Shema and its mitzvot (commandments) "surround" us: People tend to be drawn to materialism and give in to their lusts by following foolish, worldly pleasures. We need constant reminders that we are part of God's Cabinet and have responsibilities to Him. Without these reminders, we can't keep focused on what God put us here to do. His lovingkindness determined that we should say the Shema twice a day to help us stay on track spiritually.

The general purpose of any mitzvah is to preserve and heighten our spiritual wholesomeness and to attach us to God. Saying the Shema reminds us that our thoughts, speech, and actions affect the entire universe. That, in turn, encourages us to live with ongoing devotion and fervor in our service to the Almighty.

The Shema also refocuses us at least twice a day so that we are not derailed by constant exposure to forces that negate our spirituality. The Shema can help us regain our spiritual bearings and infuse us with tremendous spiritual energy only if we appreciate and concentrate on what we are saying.

HOLOCAUST MEMORIES

During World War Two, countless Jewish parents gave their precious children to Christian neighbors and orphanages in the hope that the latter would provide safe havens for them. The parents expected that they, or their relatives, would take these children back if they survived the war. The few parents who did not perish in the Holocaust, and were able to reclaim their children, often faced another horror. While the parents had summoned the strength to survive the slave labor and death camps, or had hidden out for years, those who took their children were busy teaching them the ways of other religions.

[Additionally,] many Jewish children who were taken in by orphanages, convents and the like, had no parents or close relatives left after the Holocaust. When rabbis or distant relatives finally tracked down many of these children, the priests and nuns who had been their caretakers insisted that no children from Jewish homes were in their institutions. Thus, countless Jewish children were not only stripped of their entire families, they were also stripped of their souls.

In May 1945, Rabbi Eliezer Silver from the United States and Dayan Grunfeld from England were sent as chaplains to liberate some of the death camps. While there, they were told that many Jewish children had been placed in a monastery in Alsace-Lorraine. The rabbis went there to reclaim them.

When they approached the priest in charge, they asked that the Jewish children be released into the rabbis' care. "I'm sorry," the priest responded, "but there is no way of knowing which children here came from Jewish families. You must have documentation if you wish me to do what you ask."

Of course, the kind of documentation that the priest wanted was unobtainable at the end of the war. The rabbis asked to see the list of names of children who were in the monastery. As the rabbis read the list, they pointed to those that belonged to Jewish children. "I'm sorry," the priest insisted, "but the names that you pointed to could be either Jewish or Gentile. Miller is a German name, and Markovich is a Russian name, and Swersky is a Polish name. You can't prove that these are Jewish children. If you can't prove which children are Jewish, and do it very quickly, you will have to leave." One of the rabbis had a brilliant idea. "We'd like to come back again this evening when you are putting the children to sleep."

The priest reluctantly agreed.

That evening the rabbis came to the dormitory, where row upon row of little beds were arranged. The children, many of whom had been in the monastery since the war started in 1939, were going to sleep. The rabbis walked through the aisles of beds, calling out, "Shema Yisrael—Hear, Israel, the Lord is our God, the Lord is One!" One by one, children burst into tears and shrieked, "Mommy!" "Maman!" "Momma!" "Mamushka!" in each of their native tongues. The priest had succeeded in teaching these precious Jewish souls about the Trinity, the New Testament, and the Christian savior. Each child knew how to say Mass. But the priest did not succeed in erasing these children's memories of their Jewish mothers—now murdered—putting them to bed every night with the Shema on their lips. *(Thanks to Miriam Swerdlov for the story.)*

STAYING FOCUSED

It is natural to find "too much" religiosity oppressive if we do mitzvot mechanically, or see them merely as "brownie points" to be accumulated. The true purpose of life is to develop our relationship with the Almighty such that we experience the exquisite spiritual pleasure of closeness to Him. That surpasses all other pleasures, and we create receptivity to it every time that we do a mitzvah with the right frame of mind.

By appreciating how everything we do can draw us closer to our Creator, by continually relating to Him in every part of our lives, and by doing His commandments, we can enjoy His love and nearness. Whenever we draw Him out of hiding in our daily lives, we make Him more apparent to ourselves and to others.

We need to say the Shema twice a day because it serves a critical spiritual function. It affirms our belief in one God who cares about, and is always involved in, the details of our personal lives. It also shows that we accept religious responsibilities. Yet there is also more to the Shema than this. We will plumb its depths by first exploring the basic philosophical concepts that underlie it.

SIMPLE TRUTHS

—

Lesson Three

CREATION REVISITED

INTRODUCTION—
A THOUGHT EXPERIMENT

Exercise 1

Think for a moment: What if you knew that nothing could ever go wrong? What if you believed that there can never be any such thing as randomness or chaos, that absolutely nothing has or will ever happen unless it's supposed to happen? That there is a reason, a system, a plan, and a purpose— all rooted in absolute goodness—behind every moment, event, and experience?

How would you live differently?

UNDERSTANDING CREATION
HOW IT ALL BEGAN

Text 1
GENESIS 1:1

בְּרֵאשִׁית בָּרָא אֱלֹקִים אֵת הַשָּׁמַיִם וְאֵת הָאָרֶץ.

In the beginning, God created the heavens and the earth.

Question for Discussion

What is the difference between God's act of creation and our acts of creation?

Text 2

RABBI MOSHE BEN NACHMAN, GENESIS 1:1

הַקָּדוֹשׁ בָּרוּךְ הוּא בָּרָא כָּל הַנִּבְרָאִים מֵאֲפִיסָה מֻחְלֶטֶת. וְאֵין אֶצְלֵנוּ בִּלְשׁוֹן הַקֹּדֶשׁ בְּהוֹצָאַת הַיֵּשׁ מֵאַיִן אֶלָּא לְשׁוֹן "בָּרָא". וְאֵין כָּל הַנַּעֲשֶׂה תַּחַת הַשֶּׁמֶשׁ אוֹ לְמַעְלָה, הֹוֶה מִן הָאַיִן הַתְּחָלָה רִאשׁוֹנָה.

The Holy One, blessed be He, created all of the creations from absolute nothingness. In the Holy Tongue, *bara* ("created") refers exclusively to creation *ex nihilo*. [Subsequent to the original act of creation,] nothing beneath the sun or above it emerges from nothingness.

RABBI MOSHE BEN NACHMAN (NACHMANIDES, RAMBAN)
1194–1270

Scholar, philosopher, author and physician. Nachmanides was born in Spain and served as leader of Iberian Jewry. In 1263, he was summoned by King James of Aragon to a public disputation with Pablo Cristiani, a Jewish apostate. Though Nachmanides was the clear victor of the debate, he had to flee Spain because of the resulting persecution. He moved to Israel and helped reestablish communal life in Jerusalem. He authored a classic commentary on the Pentateuch and a commentary on the Talmud.

CONTINUOUS CREATION

Question for Discussion

If God did not want something to exist, what would happen to it?

Text 3

SIDDUR, BLESSINGS OF THE *SHEMA*

נוֹרָא תְהִלּוֹת, אֲדוֹן הַנִּפְלָאוֹת, הַמְחַדֵּשׁ בְּטוּבוֹ בְּכָל יוֹם תָּמִיד מַעֲשֵׂה בְרֵאשִׁית, כָּאָמוּר, "לְעוֹשֵׂה אוֹרִים גְּדוֹלִים, כִּי לְעוֹלָם חַסְדּוֹ" (תְּהִילִים קלו, ז).

He is awesome in praise, Master of wonders. In His goodness He renews each day, continuously, the work of Creation, as it is said: "[Give thanks] to Him Who makes the great luminaries, for His kindness is eternal" (Psalms 136:7).

Text 4

RABBI YEHUDAH HALEVI, *KUZARI*, 3:11

אֵין עִנְיַן הַבְּרִיאָה דּוֹמֶה לְעִנְיַן הַמְּלָאכָה, כִּי הָאוּמָן כְּשֶׁהוּא
עוֹשֶׂה רֵחַיִים, עַל הַדִּמְיוֹן, וְיֵלֵךְ לוֹ, וְיַעֲשׂוּ הָרֵחַיִים שֶׁבַּעֲבוּרוֹ
נַעֲשׂוּ, וְהַבּוֹרֵא יִתְבָּרֵךְ בּוֹרֵא הָאֵיבָרִים וְנוֹתֵן לָהֶם כּוֹחוֹת
וּמַמְשִׁיךְ לָהֶם עִם הָרְגָעִים, וְאִילוּ הָיוּ מַעֲלִים עַל לֵב הִסְתַּלְקוּת
הַשְׁגָחָתוֹ וְהַנְהָגָתוֹ רֶגַע אֶחָד, הָיָה נִפְסָד הָעוֹלָם כּוּלוֹ.

Divine creation is not the same as human labor.
For example, when a builder builds a mill, the
mill will continue to do what it was built to do,
even after the builder goes elsewhere. However . . . were God to remove His Providence
and supervision even for one moment (if we can
imagine such a thing), the entire universe would
cease to exist.

RABBI YEHUDAH HALEVI
CA. 1075–1141

Noted author, physician, and poet.
Rabbi Yehudah Halevi is best
known as the author of the *Kuzari*,
a philosophical work, written in the
form of a discussion between a Jew,
a Christian, and a Muslim before the
King of the Khazars. In addition to the
Kuzari, he wrote thousands of poems, of
which only a few hundred survive today.

Text 5

RABBI SHNE'UR ZALMAN OF LIADI, *TANYA, SHA'AR
HAYICHUD VEHA'EMUNAH*, CH. 2

**RABBI SHNE'UR ZALMAN
OF LIADI (ALTER REBBE)**
1745–1812

Chasidic rebbe, halachic authority,
and founder of the Chabad movement.
The Alter Rebbe was born in
Liozna, Belarus, and was among the
principal students of the Magid of
Mezeritch. His numerous works
include the *Tanya*, an early classic
containing the fundamentals of
Chabad Chasidism, and *Shulchan
Aruch HaRav*, an expanded and
reworked code of Jewish law.

וְהִנֵּה, מִכַּאן תְּשׁוּבַת הַמִּינִים וְגִלּוּי שׁוֹרֶשׁ טָעוּתָם הַכּוֹפְרִים
בְּהַשְׁגָּחָה פְּרָטִית וּבְאוֹתוֹת וּמוֹפְתֵי הַתּוֹרָה, שֶׁטּוֹעִים בְּדִמְיוֹנָם
הַכּוֹזֵב שֶׁמְּדַמִּין מַעֲשֵׂה ה' עוֹשֵׂה שָׁמַיִם וָאָרֶץ לְמַעֲשֵׂה אֱנוֹשׁ
וְתַחְבּוּלוֹתָיו, כִּי כַּאֲשֶׁר יֵצֵא לְצוֹרֵף כְּלִי שׁוּב אֵין הַכְּלִי צָרִיךְ
לִידֵי הַצּוֹרֵף, כִּי אַף שֶׁיָּדָיו מְסֻלָּקוֹת הֵימֶנּוּ וְהוֹלֵךְ לוֹ בַּשּׁוּק,
הַכְּלִי קַיָּם בְּתַבְנִיתוֹ וְצַלְמוֹ מַמָּשׁ כַּאֲשֶׁר יָצָא מִידֵי הַצּוֹרֵף. כַּךְ
מְדַמִּין הַסְּכָלִים הָאֵלּוּ מַעֲשֵׂה שָׁמַיִם וָאָרֶץ.

אַךְ טָח מֵרְאוֹת עֵינֵיהֶם הַהֶבְדֵּל הַגָּדוֹל שֶׁבֵּין מַעֲשֵׂה אֱנוֹשׁ
וְתַחְבּוּלוֹתָיו, שֶׁהוּא יֵשׁ מִיֵּשׁ, רַק שֶׁמְּשַׁנֶּה הַצּוּרָה וְהַתְּמוּנָה
מִתְּמוּנַת חֲתִיכַת כֶּסֶף לִתְמוּנַת כְּלִי, לְמַעֲשֵׂה שָׁמַיִם וָאָרֶץ
שֶׁהוּא יֵשׁ מֵאַיִן. וְהוּא פֶּלֶא גָּדוֹל יוֹתֵר מִקְּרִיעַת יַם סוּף עַל
דֶּרֶךְ מָשָׁל, שֶׁהוֹלִיךְ ה' אֶת הַיָּם בְּרוּחַ קָדִים עַזָּה כָּל הַלַּיְלָה
וַיִּבָּקְעוּ הַמַּיִם, וְנִצְבוּ כְּמוֹ נֵד וּכְחוֹמָה, וְאִילּוּ הִפְסִיק ה' אֶת
הָרוּחַ כְּרֶגַע, הָיוּ הַמַּיִם חוֹזְרִים וְנִיגָּרִים בְּמוֹרָד כְּדַרְכָּם וְטִבְעָם
וְלֹא קָמוּ כְּחוֹמָה בְּלִי סָפֵק, אַף שֶׁהַטֶּבַע הַזֶּה בְּמַיִם גַּם כֵּן נִבְרָא
וּמְחוּדָשׁ יֵשׁ מֵאַיִן, שֶׁהֲרֵי חוֹמַת אֲבָנִים נִצֶּבֶת מֵעַצְמָהּ בְּלִי רוּחַ
רַק שֶׁטֶּבַע הַמַּיִם אֵינוֹ כֵּן.

וְכָל שֶׁכֵּן וְקַל וָחוֹמֶר בִּבְרִיאַת יֵשׁ מֵאַיִן, שֶׁהִיא לְמַעְלָה מֵהַטֶּבַע
וְהַפְּלֵא וָפֶלֶא יוֹתֵר מִקְּרִיעַת יַם סוּף, עַל אַחַת כַּמָּה וְכַמָּה
שֶׁבְּהִסְתַּלְּקוּת כֹּחַ הַבּוֹרֵא מִן הַנִּבְרָא חַס וְשָׁלוֹם, יָשׁוּב הַנִּבְרָא
לְאַיִן וָאֶפֶס מַמָּשׁ. אֶלָּא צָרִיךְ לִהְיוֹת כֹּחַ הַפּוֹעֵל בַּנִּפְעָל תָּמִיד
לְהַחֲיוֹתוֹ וּלְקַיְּימוֹ.

They err, making a false analogy in compar-
ing the work of God, the Creator of heaven and
earth, to the work of man and his schemes. For,
when a smith has made a vessel, that vessel is no
longer dependent on the smith, and even when
his hands are removed from it and he goes away,
the vessel remains in exactly the same image and
form as when it left his hands. Those who lack

intelligence conceive of the creation of heaven and earth in the same way.

But their eyes are covered, [preventing them from] seeing the great difference between the work of man and his schemes—which consists of making one thing out of another which already exists, merely changing the form and appearance from an ingot of silver to a vessel—and the making of heaven and earth, which is *ex nihilo,* an even greater miracle than, for example, the splitting of the Red Sea. For then, God drove back the sea by way of a strong east wind the entire night, causing the waters to divide and stand upright as a wall. If God had stopped the wind, the waters would have instantly flowed downward, as is their way and nature. Undoubtedly, they would not have continued to stand upright as a wall, even though the nature of water [to flow downward] is also created *ex nihilo,* for a stone wall stands erect by itself without the assistance of the wind, but the nature of water is not so.

[If the continuous action of God was necessary for the splitting of the Red Sea,] how much more so [is it necessary] in the creation of existence out of nothing—which transcends nature and is far more miraculous than the splitting of the Red Sea. Certainly, if the power of the Creator would withdraw from the thing created, God forbid, that thing would revert to naught and complete non-existence. Rather, the activating force of the Creator must *continuously* be in the thing created to give it life and existence.

Figure 3.1

The Differences between Divine
Creation and Human Creation

Human Creation	Divine Creation
Human beings create from existing materials and ideas.	God creates from absolute nothingness.
After a person creates, the creation continues to exist on its own, without requiring the creator's involvement.	God must continually create existence— otherwise all would revert to nothingness.

FOR GOODNESS' SAKE

Text 6

RABBI CHAIM VITAL, *ETS CHAYIM, SHA'AR HAKELALIM*

כְּשֶׁעָלָה בִּרְצוֹנוֹ יִתְבָּרֵךְ שְׁמוֹ לִבְרוֹא אֶת הָעוֹלָם, כְּדֵי לְהֵיטִיב
לִבְרוּאָיו וְיַכִּירוּ גְדוּלָתוֹ, וְיִזְכּוּ לִהְיוֹת מֶרְכָּבָה לְמַעְלָה לְהִדָּבֵק
בּוֹ יִתְ׳ . . .

When it arose in His will, blessed be His Name, to create the world in order to do good to His creatures, that they might recognize His greatness and merit to be a vehicle for that which is above, and to bond with Him. . . .

OPENING THE FLOOR

Exercise 2

What are some practical and personally relevant implications of the concept of perpetual creation? Fill in the chart below.

	Before understanding perpetual creation I might have thought that . . .	**After understanding perpetual creation I realize that . . .**
1		
2		
3		
4		
5		
6		
7		
8		

THE IMPLICATIONS
OF PERPETUAL CREATION
AVOIDING ANXIETY

Exercise 3

List three stressful events that you recently experienced. Rate the level of anxiety that you felt as a result of each scenario on a scale from 1 to 4.

Stressful event	Rating

---

1) no anxiety, 2) a little anxiety, 3) manageable anxiety, 4) unmanageable anxiety

Text 7

SCOTT STOSSEL, "SURVIVING ANXIETY," *THE ATLANTIC*, JANUARY/FEBRUARY 2014

Anxiety and its associated disorders represent the most common form of officially classified mental illness in the United States today, more common even than depression and other mood disorders. According to the National Institute of Mental Health, some 40 million American adults, about one in six, are suffering from some kind of anxiety disorder at any given time; based on the most recent data from the Department of Health and Human Services, their treatment accounts for more than a quarter of all spending on mental-health care. Recent epidemiological data suggest that one in four of us can expect to be stricken by debilitating anxiety at some point in our lifetime. . . .

And anxiety, of course, extends far beyond the population of the officially mentally ill. In a much-cited 1976 study, primary-care physicians reported that anxiety was one of the most frequent complaints driving patients to their offices—more frequent than the common cold. Almost everyone alive has at some point experienced the torments of anxiety—or of fear or of stress or of worry, which are distinct but related phenomena.

SCOTT STOSSEL

1969-

American journalist and editor. Stossel is the editor of *The Atlantic* magazine, and previously served as executive editor of *The American Prospect* magazine. In 2014, Stossel was awarded the Erikson Institute Prize for Excellence in Mental Health Media. Stossel is the author of *Sarge: The Life and Times of Sargent Shriver* and *My Age of Anxiety*.

Text 8

DAVID ROCK, *YOUR BRAIN AT WORK* (NEW YORK: HARPERBUSINESS, 2009), PP. 120–121

The brain craves certainty... Think of the brain as a prediction machine. Massive neuronal resources are devoted to predicting what will happen each moment.... The brain likes to know what is going on by recognizing patterns in the world. It likes to feel certain....

Entire industries are devoted to resolving larger uncertainties: from shop-front palm readers, to the mythical "black boxes" that can supposedly predict stock trends and make investors millions. Some parts of accounting and consulting make their money by helping executives experience a perception of increasing certainty, through strategic planning and "forecasting." While the financial markets of 2008 showed once again that the future is inherently uncertain, the one thing that's certain is that people will always pay lots of money at least to *feel* less uncertain. That's because uncertainty feels, to the brain, like a threat to your life.

DAVID ROCK

Dr. David Rock is the Director of the NeuroLeadership Institute, a global initiative bringing neuroscientists and leadership experts together to build a new science for leadership development. He is the author of the business best-seller *Your Brain at Work,* as well as *Quiet Leadership* and the textbook *Coaching with the Brain in Mind.* He blogs for the *Harvard Business Review, Fortune Magazine, Psychology Today* and the *Huffington Post.*

Text 9

"BROKEN DREAMS," AUTHOR UNKNOWN

As children bring their broken toys
With tears for us to mend,
I brought my broken dreams to God
Because He was my friend.

But then instead of leaving Him
In peace to work alone,
I hung around and tried to help
With ways that were my own.

At last I snatched them back and cried,
"How could you be so slow?"
"My child," He said, "What could I do?
You never did let go."

Exercise 4

In the left-hand column are negative things that people commonly say to themselves when facing stress, anxiety, and fear that undermine optimism and confidence. How would our understanding of the concepts of divine creation help us change our negative thought pattern to a healthier, more positive one? Fill in the chart below.

Negative thought	A thought we can replace it with (based on the notion of perpetual creation and God's goodness)
"It's impossible."	
"I can't go on."	
"I'm not able."	
"I'm afraid."	
"I feel all alone."	

SEIZING THE MOMENT

Text 10

THE REBBE, RABBI MENACHEM M. SCHNEERSON,
TORAT MENACHEM 5742, 3:1217

לְכָל רֶגַע שֶׁנִּיתַּן לָאָדָם יֵשׁ תַּכְלִית מְסוּיֶּימֶת – כְּדֵי שֶׁהָאָדָם
יְמַלֵּא אֶת שְׁלִיחוּתוֹ שֶׁל הַקָּדוֹשׁ בָּרוּךְ הוּא הַמּוּטֶלֶת עָלָיו
לְקַיֵּים בְּרֶגַע זֶה (בְּהֶתְאֵם לַכְּלָל דְּ"אָדָם לְעָמָל יוּלָּד"(איוב
ה, ז), שֶׁאָז נַעֲשֶׂה רֶגַע זֶה לִמְצִיאוּת בַּעֲלַת תּוֹכֶן וּמַשְׁמָעוּת
אֲמִיתִּית – תּוֹכֶן הַקֶּשֶׁר עִם הַקָּדוֹשׁ בָּרוּךְ הוּא, שֶׁהוּא בָּרָא
אֶת הַמְּצִיאוּת דְּרֶגַע זֶה, כְּיָדוּעַ תּוֹרַת הַמַּגִּיד שֶׁכְּלָלוּת מְצִיאוּת
הַזְּמַן הוּא נִבְרָא כְּכָל הַנִּבְרָאִים.

זֹאת אוֹמֶרֶת: מֵאַחֵר שֶׁהַקָּדוֹשׁ בָּרוּךְ הוּא בּוֹרֵא עַתָּה אֶת
הַמְּצִיאוּת דְּרֶגַע זֶה . . . וְיֶשְׁנוֹ כְּלָל שֶׁ"לֹא בָּרָא הַקָּדוֹשׁ בָּרוּךְ
הוּא בְּעוֹלָמוֹ דָּבָר אֶחָד לְבַטָּלָה" (שבת עז, ב) – הֵטִיל הַקָּדוֹשׁ
בָּרוּךְ הוּא עַל הָאָדָם שְׁלִיחוּת מְיוּחֶדֶת: לְקַשֵּׁר אֶת מְצִיאוּת
הָרֶגַע (שֶׁהוּא חֵלֶק מֵהֶמְשֵׁךְ הַזְּמַן) עִם מַעֲשֶׂה טוֹב שֶׁנַּעֲשֶׂה
בְּרֶגַע זֶה.

וְלָכֵן, כַּאֲשֶׁר עוֹבֵר רֶגַע מְסוּיָּים שֶׁהָאָדָם אֵינוֹ מְנַצְּלוֹ לַעֲשִׂיַּית
מַעֲשֶׂה טוֹב – הֲרֵי הוּא מְאַבֵּד אֶת כְּלָלוּת הַמְּצִיאוּת דְּרֶגַע זֶה!

**RABBI MENACHEM
MENDEL SCHNEERSON**
1902–1994

The towering Jewish leader of the 20th
century, known as "the Lubavitcher
Rebbe," or simply as "the Rebbe." Born
in southern Ukraine, the Rebbe escaped
Nazi-occupied Europe, arriving in
the U.S. in June 1941. The Rebbe
inspired and guided the revival of
traditional Judaism after the European
devastation, impacting virtually
every Jewish community the world
over. The Rebbe often emphasized
that the performance of just one
additional good deed could usher
in the era of Mashiach. The Rebbe's
scholarly talks and writings have been
printed in more than 200 volumes.

Every moment God grants a person has a specific purpose. That purpose is actualized when a person fulfills the mission that God has ordained for him or her for that moment (following the truism that "man is born to labor"), causing that moment to become truly meaningful and substantive. The moment then becomes infused with divine purpose, and visibly connected to its Creator. For, as the Maggid [Rabbi Dov Ber of Mezeritch] teaches us, time itself is a creation like all other of God's creations.

God is creating, right now, the reality of this moment . . . and it is axiomatic that "God created nothing in His world in vain." It follows then that the existence of this moment implies that God has given us a unique mission: to connect the existence of the moment (which is one part of the continuum of time) with a good deed that will be done at that moment.

Therefore, when a moment passes by which a person did not use to do a good deed, this person has wasted the entirety of the purpose of that moment!

OBLITERATING OBSTACLES

Text 11

THE REBBE, RABBI MENACHEM M. SCHNEERSON, *LIKUTEI SICHOT* 7:52

דֶער **אויבֶּערְשְׁטֶער** אִיז שְׁטֶענְדִיק מְהַוֶּה דִי בְּרִיאָה מֵאַיִן לְיֵשׁ, אוּן דִי כַּוָּונַת הַבְּרִיאָה אִיז בִּשְׁבִיל יִשְׂרָאֵל וּבִשְׁבִיל הַתּוֹרָה – קֶען בְּמֵילָא נִיט זַיין קֵיין מְצִיאוּת אִין דֶער בְּרִיאָה . . . וָואס זָאל שְׁטֶערְן צוּ תּוֹרָה וּמִצְוֹת (אַז דֶער מֶענְטשׁ זָאל **נִיט קֶענֶען** מְקַיֵּים זַיין אַ מִצְוָה וָואס עֶר דַאַרְף מְקַיֵּים זַיין – אֲפִילוּ וֶוען עֶר וֶועט אִיר **וֶועלֹן** מְקַיֵּים זַיין.

God is continually creating existence out of nothing, and the intent of creation is for our sake and for the sake of the Torah. It follows that there can be no reality in creation that can obstruct

Torah and *mitzvot* such that a person who wants to fulfill them is unable to do so.

Exercise 5

1. Identify one idea you will think about next time you are faced with anxiety, fear, doubt, or worry.

2. Identify one small step you will take to use your time more productively, with the recognition that every moment contains Godly potential.

3. Identify one small step you will take to overcome an obstacle you currently perceive to performing a mitzvah, with the recognition that there can never be a circumstance that prevents us from fulfilling our divine purpose.

My Personal Take

In the space provided below, write down, in your own words, the simple truth you learned in today's lesson.

בְּרֵאשִׁית בָּרָא אֱלֹקִים In the beginning, God created אֵת הַשָּׁמַיִם וְאֵת הָאָרֶץ. the heavens and the earth.

Key Points

1. While human creation involves forming things from existing materials or conceptual principles, divine creation is *ex nihilo*—something from nothing.

2. God's creation *ex nihilo* is not a one-time act; rather, God continually creates the world, willing it out of a state of utter nothingness into existence at every single moment.

3. Because God must constantly will existence into being, absent God's desire or will for something to exist, it simply would not exist.

4. God's creating and constant animation of the universe is rooted in God's absolute *chesed*, goodness and kindness.

5. The notion of continuous divine creation is the ultimate response to anxiety, for true peace of mind comes from knowing that there is a reason, a plan, and a purpose—all rooted in absolute goodness—behind every event and experience.

6. Continuous divine creation implies that every moment is meaningful and important. No moment is created in vain; rather, every moment we are granted has a divinely ordained purpose.

7. The notion of divine creation teaches us that God would never create a situation that makes it impossible for us to carry out His will. Therefore, there can never be a circumstance that prevents us from fulfilling our divine purpose.

APPENDIX

Exercise

Think of someone you trust: What qualities does this person have?

	Qualities	Why is this important for gaining trust?
1		
2		
3		
4		
5		
6		
7		

Ephraim Wuensch, 2016

Where Is G-d? Or Where Is G-d Not?

By Rabbi Yosef Marcus

A Chasidic lumber merchant in Riga was calculating his accounts. Under a column of figures he inadvertently wrote, "Total: Ein od milvado— *There is none besides Him!" In response to his assistant's raised eyebrow, he said: "During prayer it is considered perfectly natural to let one's mind wander off to one's lumber in Riga. So what is so surprising if in the middle of business dealings the mind is invaded by thoughts of the unity of G-d?"* —Chasidic Story

It is perhaps the most oft-quoted phrase in Chabad Chasidism: *ein od milvado*—there is none besides Him. It is a three-word phrase that encapsulates an entire philosophy. It is a notion that every *chasid* strives to absorb. In its common interpretation, the phrase expresses the fundamental Jewish belief that there is no other god besides Him. Monotheism. It expresses the same idea as "Hear O Israel, the L-rd is our G-d, the L-rd is one."

But in Chabad philosophy, the phrase means much more. Not only is there no other *god* besides Him, there is *nothing* besides Him— literally. Only G-d exists. This is a statement on the nature of the cosmos as much as it is a theological belief. What of the world and all that is in it? What of the empirical sightings of our fleshly eye? Is it only an illusion?

No. The Torah states clearly: *In the beginning G-d created the heaven and the earth.* For six days He created things. These things exist really, for if the world is not real, then Torah, indeed life itself, is meaningless. Such a notion is untenable. How then to reconcile our perception of reality with *ein od milvado*? The Alter Rebbe, Rabbi Schneur Zalman of Liadi, founder of Chabad Chasidism, explains it this way (*Shaar Hayichud v'haEmunah* III):

If the eye were allowed to perceive the life and spirit that is in every created being—which courses within it from the utterance of G-d's mouth—then the corporeality and tangibility of the created being would not be perceived by our eyes at all. For it is literally null in relation to the life and spirit that it contains, since without the spirit it is literally naught, a nonentity, as it was before the Six Days of Creation. The spirit that flows to it from the mouth of G-d is the only thing that removes it constantly from nothingness and brings it into being.

It follows, then, that there is nothing besides Him—truly. The Alter Rebbe establishes that the world and all its contents exist only by virtue of the fact that G-d is constantly creating them. Were He for one moment to cease creating, all of creation would lose its existence. It would not crumble, or burn up, or dissolve—it would simply cease to exist, as if it had never existed.

PERPETUAL CREATION

Forever, O G-d, Your word stands firm in the heavens, says the psalmist.[1] The Baal Shem Tov would cite the Midrash[2]: *Your words that you spoke, "Let there be a firmament"—these words continue to stand in the heavens to create them.* And just as words exist only as long as they are being uttered, so the world, created by G-d's mouth, must be constantly uttered into existence.

For the existence of the world—created from nothing— was and is a miracle. It was and is "unnatural." And just as we don't expect miracles to go on indefinitely—we expect the waters of the sea to return to their natural flow after G-d is finished holding them up for the Israelites—so should we not expect the world to continue to exist. We should expect it to return to its natural state: nonexistence.

When you throw a rock in the air, you don't expect it to stay there. As soon as the power of your throw invested in the rock dissipates, the rock returns to its natural state: inert. So, yes, the world exists. But its existence is entirely

---

1. Psalms 119:89.
2. *Midrash Tehillim* on the verse.

dependent upon the Divine word that commands its existence.

Such "existence" cannot compete with *true* existence, one that is not dependent on any other being: the absolute existence of G-d. The existence of the world is not self-attributable. Even as it exists, it is not truly existent—just as the airborne rock has not become "a flying rock." The world does not take on the properties of existence even as it exists. Maimonides says as much in the second chapter of his "Fundamentals of Torah":

This is what the prophet means with "G-d is true." He alone is true, and no other being possesses truth like His truth. This is what the Torah says: *ein od milvado*—i.e., there is no other *true* existence besides Him that is like Him.

This doctrine of "perpetual creation" provided a rational foundation to the Baal Shem Tov's motto: G-d is everywhere. His opponents argued, How can you put G-d in the trash bin? The Alter Rebbe said, How can a trash bin exist without a Divine directive invested in it?[3]

Before and during prayer the Chabad *chasid* will meditate on *ein od milvado*. He will contemplate the words of the *Zohar*: *No place is devoid of Him*. G-d is immanent. He will break into song about it in the late hours of a *farbrengen*. He will spend his entire lifetime internalizing this notion—a notion that runs contrary to his sensory perception.

This is his task.

ROOSTER'S CROW

Each of the Chabad masters had a particular discourse that he would repeat every two or three years. This they did in order to "purify the environment." The recurring discourse of the fourth Rebbe, Rabbi Shmuel, concerned *ein od milvado*.[4]

The present discourse entitled *Who is like You* of 5629 (1869), begins with a lengthy discussion on the spiritual roots of physical phenomena. The human eye beholds what is essentially the final and lowest manifestation of supernal, spiritual phenomena. Everything in this world has its source and counterpart in the spiritual realms. The early morning crow of the rooster is a reverberation of spiritual stirrings in the supernal world of *Atzilut* and beyond. Day and night are the reflections of the two types of celestial song. (Thus Moses knew day from night during his forays into heaven.)

The Rebbe uses this concept to make sense of a number of otherwise cryptic Midrashic statements. The Midrash says[5] that G-d created the world with snow and earth from beneath the Throne of Glory. According to the Rebbe, these statements refer to the spiritual origins of physical phenomena. In like vein, Talmudic tales[6] about talking grass are understood as references to the spiritual antecedents of grass, the angels (who can certainly speak).

Myriad levels of evolvement stand between the original, spiritual form of an entity and its physical form. Yet no amount of evolvement can produce a corporeal being out of a spiritual being. Between the lowest spiritual level and the highest physical level there is still an unbridgeable gap that must be closed. This is where "something from nothing" cannot be introduced. Up until this point, each level is within the realm of the one above it—like a chain, whose every link is ultimately attached to all the links. At this point there is a break—the physical reality is not linked to its spiritual source, the source is concealed from it. There is no point of contact between them. It is this concealment that creates the physical reality. Without this concealment, the coarse physical reality would not be visible: "*the corporeality and tangibility of the created being would not be perceived by our eyes at all*." Hence is explained another mysterious statement in the Talmud[7] about G-d "extending His small finger among

3.   It should be noted that even according to Chasidic philosophy, G-d—being beyond all rational rules—could theoretically have created a world separate from Him which would at the same time not contradict *ein od milvado,* yet He chose to be perpetually involved. (see *Sefer Hamaamarim 5643*, p. 35ff; *Torat Menachem – Hadranim al Harambam v'Shas*, p. 43 ff.).

4.   *Hayom Yom* 28 Tammuz.

5.   *Pirkei d'Rabbi Eliezer*, chap. 3.

6.   Chullin 60a.

7.   Sanhedrin 38b.

the angels and consuming them." According to the Rebbe, this refers to G-d revealing more of their origins than they can handle. This revelation causes them to lose their existence. In fact all of existence will reach this state of nonexistence in the "millennia of destruction" mentioned in the Talmud.[8]

At that point, Divine revelation will be such that physical reality will cease to exist. Thus, the Rebbe concludes, even now the world is not truly existent. For true existence is everlasting. (The Rebbe cites a halachic corollary to this concept: A body of water that dries up once in seven years does not have the halachic status of "living (running) water"—even while it is running. A temporary existence is not true existence.)

FOUR ELEMENTS

The Rebbe then takes it a step further. Physical entities are not physical. Each physical entity is made up of four[9] elements: fire, water, air and earth. But its being is none of the four. Its being is the power of amalgamation that fuses the four elements into a physical being. And what is that power? The Divine "word." Isolate each of the elements and you are left with nothing.

ONE AND ONLY

The Chabad conception of *ein od milvado*, the Rebbe continues, also accounts for the use of the word *echad*, "one," in the verse *Hear O Israel, the L-rd is our G-d, the L-rd is one.*[10] It would seem that the word *yachid* (single, alone) would better convey the oneness of G-d, since the word *echad* also has the connotation of "one of many."

But that is precisely why *echad* is used. The Talmud states[11] that the three letters of the word *echad* symbolize the seven heavens and one earth (alluded to in the **ch**et—numerically equivalent to eight—of *e**ch**ad*), the four corners of the world (alluded to in the *dalet* (four) of *echa**d***), and the One G-d, Master of all (alluded to in the *alef*, which connotes rulership). So the use of the word *echad* intimates that even in the realm of many—the seven heavens and one earth, and the four corners of the world, G-d is still the only one. He is not just one outside of reality, *yachid*; He is one even within the context of supposed otherness.

The eight and the four are entirely nullified to the *Alef*—the One G-d. *Ein od milvado.*

---

8.   Sanhedrin 97a.

9.   See *Likkutei Sichot,* vol. 38, p. 184.

10.   Deuteronomy 6:4.

11.   Berachot 13b.

Juice

By Rabbi Yanki Tauber

The amazing thing was how quickly it happened. Within minutes, hundreds of millions of light bulbs, air conditioners, microwave ovens, computers, refrigerators, phone systems, traffic lights, cash registers, subway cars and blowdryers died. Ceased. Stopped. Just like that. Actually, it didn't take any time at all to happen. Because nothing happened. Rather, it stopped happening. The flow of electricity, which modern life had grown so dependent upon, stopped flowing. The delicate equilibrium of ebb and flow which enables the transmission of the electric energy from one geographical point to another was somehow disrupted, and thousands of cities went dark, one by one.

Luminance, movement and artificial thought do not come naturally to the light bulb, subway car and computer. Essentially, these are just variously shaped and joined pieces of plastic, metal and glass. It's only that they've been ingeniously designed and constructed in such a way that a current of electricity passing through them makes then perform a variety of complex—and very useful—tasks. But even as they perform these tasks, they remain dark, dumb and immobile bits of matter. They're not really acting—they're being acted upon by the current of energy that's "enlivening" them. The moment this external acting force ceases to act, these objects will simply revert to their natural state. The subway car becomes a waiting room and the computer becomes a desk ornament.

When the juice stopped flowing in the cities of the Northeast, we weren't just set back 150 years. A century-and-a-half ago we got along just fine without electrical appliances. In 2003, we had to learn all over again to accept the temperature of the atmosphere on a summer evening, make do with more humble sources of light, use our own two feet as a means of transportation, and do our computing with a naked human mind, aided, at most, with pencil and paper.

But imagine that life itself ran on electricity. That the engine of our heart, the RAM and ROM of our brain, the force fields that pull together countless billions of cells, atoms and quarks into a "body," the surges of will and desire that form the core of our "self" —were all wired to one huge "power station." Imagine that we lived with the awareness that, in every instant of time, we were utterly dependent upon this outside power source for existence and life. That our existence and life were not inherent qualities that we somehow "possess", but are acted upon us by that external energy source, and that the moment that source should cease to so act, we would simply cease.

That, in fact, is how the founder of Chabad Chassidism, Rabbi Schneur Zalman of Liadi (1745-1812), describes the entirety of creation. All of existence, explains Rabbi Schneur Zalman, was created by G-d *ex nihilo* ("something from nothing"). Since "something from nothing" is an absolute impossibility, this means that the essential nature of our existence remains "nothing"; our somethingness is a quality that must be *constantly* imposed upon us by an outside force that is beyond both "something" and "nothing" (for indeed He created both notions) and can thus manipulate them both, imposing the one upon the other. G-d's creation of the world, therefore, was not a one-time act. G-d constantly "speaks" the world into being, exactly as He did the very first time He uttered "Let there be . . ." "If the letters," writes Rabbi Schneur Zalman, "of the Ten Utterances by which the earth was created during the Six Days of Creation were to depart from it for an instant, G-d forbid, it would revert to naught and absolute nothingness, exactly as before the Six Days of Creation" (*Tanya*, part II, ch. 1).

A frightening thought? I don't think so. In fact, the more I think about it, the more encouraging it is. What this basically means is that every nanosecond of time G-d looks upon our world, contemplates all the good and evil, kindness and cruelty, triumphs and failings, imperfections and strivings that goes on in it, and makes a conscious decision to grant it existence and life. It's as if you would ask the Creator, a billion times a second, "Seeing what's become of it, would you do it all over again?" and G-d says, "Yes, I would, exactly as it is"—and does it. If G-d sees something worthwhile there, I'm assuming that we, too, can.

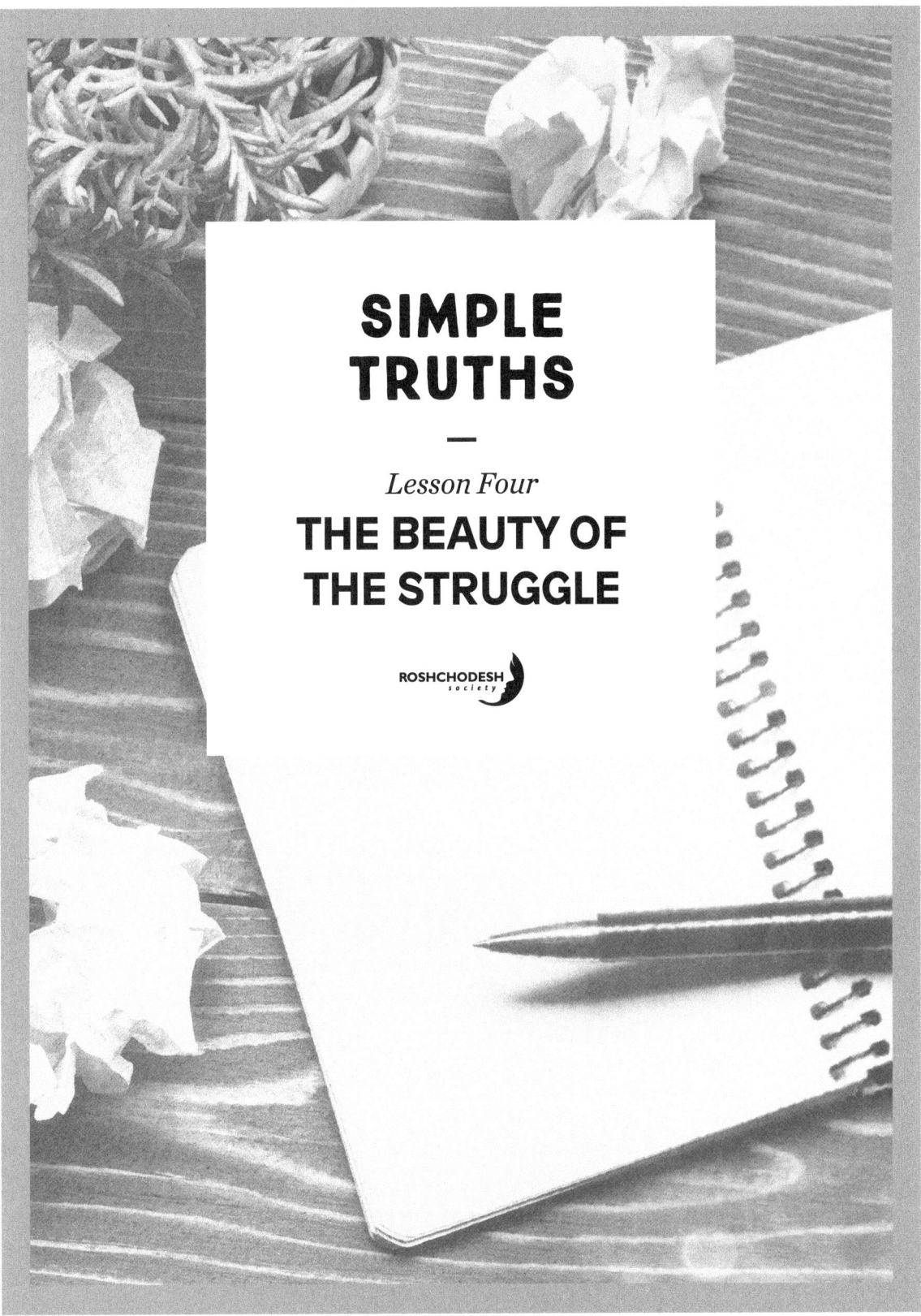

SIMPLE TRUTHS

—

Lesson Four

THE BEAUTY OF THE STRUGGLE

ROSHCHODESH
society

JOB VS. CAREER VS. CALLING

Exercise 1

Below is a list of six things that make us feel bad. Number them from 1 to 6, with "1" indicating feeling the least bad, and "6" indicating feeling the worst.

☐ Your wallet is stolen, and now you need to file a police report, get a new driver's license, and cancel your credit cards.

☐ You lose your temper and yell at your child over a minor offense, reducing him or her to tears.

☐ You break your leg in a fall, resulting in a long and painful recovery, costly medical bills, and the cancellation of your vacation plans.

☐ You mess up at work, but someone else is blamed for your mistake and gets fired for it. You lack the courage to speak up.

☐ In a moment of weakness, you do something that deeply hurts your spouse. He forgives you, but you fear that your relationship will never be the same again.

☐ A friend in need asks you for financial assistance. It is within your means to help him, but you plead poverty and turn him down.

Text 1

AMY WRZESNIEWSKI, PHD, ET AL., "JOBS, CAREERS, AND CALLINGS: PEOPLE'S RELATIONS TO THEIR WORK," *JOURNAL OF RESEARCH IN PERSONALITY* 31 (1997), P. 22

[T]here are three distinct relations people can have to their work: as Jobs, Careers, and Callings. The distinctions, drawn starkly, are these:

People who have Jobs are only interested in the material benefits from work and do not seek or receive any other type of reward from it. The work is not an end in itself, but instead is a means that allows individuals to acquire the resources needed to enjoy their time away from the Job. The major interests and ambitions of Job holders are not expressed through their work.

In contrast, people who have Careers have a deeper personal investment in their work and mark their achievements not only through monetary gain, but through advancement within the occupational structure. This advancement often brings higher social standing, increased power within the scope of one's occupation, and higher self-esteem for the worker.

Finally, people with Callings find that their work is inseparable from their life. A person with a Calling works not for financial gain or Career advancement, but instead for the fulfillment that doing the work brings to the individual. The word "calling" was originally used in a religious context, as people were understood to be "called" by God to do morally and socially significant work. While the modern sense of "calling" may have lost its religious connection . . . work that

AMY WRZESNIEWSKI, PHD

Associate professor of organizational behavior at Yale School of Management. Wrzesniewski's research interests focus on how people make meaning of their work in difficult contexts, and on the experience of work as a job, career, or calling.

people feel called to do is usually seen as socially valuable—an end in itself—involving activities that may, but need not be, pleasurable.

Exercise 2

Based on the above text, label each of the following scenarios as describing a Job, Career, or Calling:

Scenario A

Ms. A basically enjoys her work, but does not expect to be in her current job five years from now. Instead, she plans to move on to a better, higher level job. She has several goals for her future pertaining to the positions she would eventually like to hold. Sometimes her work seems a waste of time, but she knows that she must do sufficiently well in her current position in order to move on. Ms. A can't wait to get a promotion.

Job, Career, or Calling?

Scenario B

Ms. B works primarily to earn enough money to support her life outside of her job. Ms. B's job is basically a necessity of life, a lot like breathing or sleeping. She often wishes the time would pass more quickly at work. She greatly anticipates weekends and vacations. If Ms. B lived her life over again, she probably would not go into the same line of work. She would not encourage her friends and children to enter her line of work. Ms. B is very eager to retire.

Job, Career, or Calling?

Scenario C

Ms. C's work is one of the most important parts of her life.... It is one of the first things she tells people about herself.... Ms. C feels good about her work because she loves it, and because she thinks it makes the world a better place. She would encourage her friends and children to enter her line of work. Ms. C would be pretty upset if she were forced to stop working, and she is not particularly looking forward to retirement.

Job, Career, or Calling?

Question for Discussion

How do you view your struggles with your character flaws and distasteful impulses?

A. Job

B. Career

C. Calling

THE PERFECT PERSON AND THE PERPETUAL STRUGGLER

Text 2
TALMUD, YOMA 38B

רָאָה הַקָּדוֹשׁ בָּרוּךְ הוּא שֶׁצַּדִּיקִים מוּעָטִין, עָמַד וּשְׁתָלָן בְּכָל דּוֹר וָדוֹר.

God saw that *tsadikim* are few, so He planted [a few of] them in every generation.

BABYLONIAN TALMUD

A literary work of monumental proportions that draws upon the legal, spiritual, intellectual, ethical, and historical traditions of Judaism. The 37 tractates of the Babylonian Talmud contain the teachings of the Jewish sages from the period after the destruction of the 2nd Temple through the 5th century CE. It has served as the primary vehicle for the transmission of the Oral Law and the education of Jews over the centuries; it is the entry point for all subsequent legal, ethical, and theological Jewish scholarship.

Text 3
RABBI ADIN EVEN-ISRAEL (STEINSALTZ), *OPENING THE TANYA* (HOBOKEN, NJ: JOSSEY-BASS, 2003), P. 5

The introduction of the concept of the intermediate is doubtless the essential innovation of the *Tanya*. Although it is not a new term, it appears here in a new connotation and spells a fundamental departure from the basic premises of most systems of the moral teaching (*mussar*).

The aim of the *mussar* books, and the ideal to which they strive to elevate the human being, is the ideal of the *tzaddik*, "the perfectly righteous individual"; in contrast, *Tanya* was written for intermediates, for those who have not attained the station of *tzaddik*, though they are not transgressors (*resha'im,* "wicked persons") . . .

RABBI ADIN EVEN-ISRAEL (STEINSALTZ)
1937–

Talmudist, author, and philosopher. Rabbi Even-Israel Steinsaltz is considered one of the foremost Jewish thinkers of the 20th century. Praised by *Time* magazine as a "once-in-a-millennium scholar," he has been awarded the Israel Prize for his contributions to Jewish study. He lives in Jerusalem and is the founder of the Israel Institute for Talmudic Publications, a society dedicated to the translation and elucidation of the Talmud.

The persona of the *beinoni* acquires new definition. The intermediate person is not merely the median, the halfway point between utter evil and utter goodness . . . the *beinoni* is in a class alone. The *mussar* books that discussed this rank saw it as a temporary stage that one must surpass, as a spiritual dissonance to be stabilized and resolved. But the *Tanya* sees the state of *beinoni* as a legitimate, ongoing one, describing a person whose inner essence and spiritual path is the subject of a lifelong struggle—a struggle that might never reach decisive resolution. . . .

Unlike the *tzaddik*, who is in a state of constant stability, the *beinoni's* state is not inherently stable. We can say that the *Tanya's* purpose is to show the *beinoni* how to maintain balance, how to remain in a state where, although the temptation to do wrong exists, one does not sin—neither in deed, word, nor thought.

Question for Discussion

Why would God make us struggle?

THE KABBALAH OF IMPERFECTION

Text 4

RABBI SHNE'UR ZALMAN OF LIADI, *TANYA*, CHAPTER 36

וְהִנֵּה תַּכְלִית הִשְׁתַּלְשְׁלוּת הָעוֹלָמוֹת וִירִידָתָם מִמַּדְרֵגָה לְמַדְרֵגָה, אֵינוֹ בִּשְׁבִיל עוֹלָמוֹת הָעֶלְיוֹנִים, הוֹאִיל וְלָהֶם יְרִידָה מֵאוֹר פָּנָיו יִתְבָּרֵךְ. אֶלָּא הַתַּכְלִית הוּא עוֹלָם הַזֶּה הַתַּחְתּוֹן.

Now, the purpose of the evolution of the worlds, and their descent from level to level, is not for the sake of the higher worlds, since for them, this is a descent from the luminance of the divine. Rather, the purpose is this lowly world.

RABBI SHNE'UR ZALMAN OF LIADI (ALTER REBBE)
1745–1812

Chasidic rebbe, halachic authority, and founder of the Chabad movement. The Alter Rebbe was born in Liozna, Belarus, and was among the principal students of the Magid of Mezeritch. His numerous works include the *Tanya*, an early classic containing the fundamentals of Chabad Chasidism, and *Shulchan Aruch HaRav*, an expanded and reworked code of Jewish law.

Text 5

IBID.

שֶׁכַּךְ עָלָה בִּרְצוֹנוֹ יִתְבָּרֵךְ, לִהְיוֹת נַחַת רוּחַ לְפָנָיו יִתְבָּרֵךְ, כַּד אִתְכַּפְיָא סִטְרָא אַחֲרָא וְאִתְהֲפֵךְ חֲשׁוֹכָא לִנְהוֹרָא.

For so it arose in God's desire: that He should derive satisfaction when the "other side" is conquered, and darkness is transformed into light.

Text 6

IBID., CHAPTER 27

וּשְׁנֵי מִינֵי נַחַת רוּחַ לְפָנָיו יִתְבָּרֵךְ לְמַעְלָה:

אַחַת, מִבִּיטוּל הַסִּטְרָא אַחֲרָא לְגַמְרֵי, וְאִתְהַפְּכָא מְמִרִירוּ לְמִתְקָא וּמֵחֲשׁוֹכָא לִנְהוֹרָא, עַל יְדֵי הַצַּדִּיקִים.

וְהַשֵּׁנִית, כַּד אִתְכַּפְיָא הַסִּטְרָא אַחֲרָא בְּעוֹדָהּ בְּתָקְפָּהּ וּגְבוּרָתָהּ, וּמַגְבִּיהַּ עַצְמָהּ כְּנֶשֶׁר, וּמִשָּׁם מוֹרִידָהּ ה' בְּאִתְעֲרוּתָא דִלְתַתָּא עַל יְדֵי הַבֵּינוֹנִים.

There are two kinds of Divine pleasure. One [is derived] from the complete annihilation of the "other side," and the conversion of bitter to sweet and of darkness to light that is accomplished by *tsadikim*.

The second [is derived] when the "other side" is subdued while it is still at its strongest and most powerful, soaring like an eagle, and from this height, God topples it in response to human initiative. This is accomplished by *beinonim*. . . .

Text 7

IBID., CHAPTER 41

> וְהִנֵּה ה׳ נִצָּב עָלָיו, וּמְלֹא כָל הָאָרֶץ כְּבוֹדוֹ, וּמַבִּיט עָלָיו וּבוֹחֵן
> כְּלָיוֹת וָלֵב אִם עוֹבְדוֹ כָּרָאוּי.

"And, behold, God [Himself] stands over him (Genesis 28:13)," and [though] "the whole world is filled only with His Glory (Isaiah 6:3)," He studies him and "searches his innermost thoughts and emotions (Jeremiah 11:20)" to see if he is serving Him as is fitting.

OUR IMPERFECTIONS—LIABILITY, OR SOURCE OF EMPOWERMENT?

FULFILLING YOUR PART IN THE COSMIC PLAN

Question for Discussion

From a Jewish perspective, based on what we have learned, what is the ideal way to view our flaws, deficiencies, and negative character traits?

Text 8

IBID., CHAPTER 27

וְאִם הָעַצְבוּת אֵינָהּ מִדְּאָגַת עֲוֹנוֹת אֶלָּא מֵהִרְהוּרִים רָעִים וְתַאֲווֹת רָעוֹת שֶׁנּוֹפְלוֹת בְּמַחֲשַׁבְתּוֹ . . . אַדְּרַבָּה יֵשׁ לוֹ לִשְׂמֹחַ בְּחֶלְקוֹ, שֶׁאַף שֶׁנּוֹפְלוֹת לוֹ בְּמַחֲשַׁבְתּוֹ, הוּא מֵסִיחַ דַּעְתּוֹ מֵהֶן, לְקַיֵּם מַה שֶׁנֶּאֱמַר (בַּמִּדְבָּר טו, לט) "וְלֹא תָתוּרוּ אַחֲרֵי לְבַבְכֶם וְאַחֲרֵי עֵינֵיכֶם" . . .

וְאַדְּרַבָּה הָעַצְבוּת הִיא מִגַּסּוּת הָרוּחַ, שֶׁאֵינוֹ מַכִּיר מְקוֹמוֹ. וְעַל כֵּן יֵרַע לְבָבוֹ עַל שֶׁאֵינוֹ בְּמַדְרֵגַת צַדִּיק. שֶׁלְּצַדִּיקִים בְּוַדַּאי אֵין נוֹפְלִים לָהֶם הִרְהוּרֵי שְׁטוּת כְּאֵלּוּ. כִּי אִילּוּ הָיָה מַכִּיר מְקוֹמוֹ שֶׁהוּא רָחוֹק מְאֹד מִמַּדְרֵגַת צַדִּיק, וְהַלְוַאי הָיָה בֵּינוֹנִי . . . הֲרֵי זֹאת הִיא מִדַּת הַבֵּינוֹנִים וַעֲבוֹדָתָם, לִכְבּוֹשׁ הַיֵּצֶר וְהַהִרְהוּר הָעוֹלֶה מֵהַלֵּב לַמּוֹחַ.

If your despondency is not from concern over actual sins, but from negative thoughts and negative desires that befall your mind . . . then, on the contrary: you should rejoice in your lot, that although these [negative thoughts and desires] befall your consciousness, you avert your mind from them, thereby fulfilling [the divine commandment], "You shall not go astray after your heart and after your eyes . . ." (Numbers 15:39).

In fact, despondency [over such things] actually stems from conceit. [It comes from the fact] that a person does not know his place, and therefore feels bad that he is not on the level of a *tsadik*, who is not plagued by such thoughts of folly. But if he knew his place, that he is very far from the level of a *tsadik*, and that he should aspire to be a *beinoni* . . . then indeed [he would understand that] this is the character of the *beinonim* and their task in life: to subjugate the [negative] impulse and thought rising from the heart to the mind.

Text 9
IBID.

וּבְכָל דְּחִיָּה וּדְחִיָּה שֶׁמַּדְחֵהוּ מִמַּחְשַׁבְתּוֹ, אִתְכַּפְיָא סִטְרָא
אַחֲרָא לְתַתָּא. וּבְאִתְעֲרוּתָא דִּלְתַתָּא, אִתְעֲרוּתָא דִּלְעֵילָא,
וְאִתְכַּפְיָא סִטְרָא אַחֲרָא דִּלְעֵילָא ...
וּכְמוֹ שֶׁהִפְלִיג בְּזֹהַר פָּרָשַׁת תְּרוּמָה (דַּף קכח) בְּגוֹדֶל נַחַת רוּחַ
לְפָנָיו יִתְבָּרֵךְ כַּד אִתְכַּפְיָא סִטְרָא אַחֲרָא לְתַתָּא, "דְּאִסְתַּלֵּק
יְקָרָא דְּקוּדְשָׁא בְּרִיךְ הוּא לְעֵילָא עַל כּוֹלָּא, יַתִּיר מְשַׁבְּחָא
אַחֲרָא, וְאִסְתַּלְקוּתָא דָּא יַתִּיר מִכּוֹלָּא" וְכוּ'.
וְלָכֵן אַל יִפּוֹל לֵב אָדָם עָלָיו, וְלֹא יֵרַע לְבָבוֹ מְאֹד, גַּם אִם יִהְיֶה
כֵּן כָּל יָמָיו בְּמִלְחָמָה זוֹ. כִּי אוּלַי לְכַךְ נִבְרָא, וְזֹאת עֲבוֹדָתוֹ,
לְאַכַּפְיָא לְסִטְרָא אַחֲרָא תָּמִיד.

With each and every act of rejection by which a person thrusts away [the negative impulse] from his mind, the "other side" down below [in this world] is conquered; and since a "stimulus from below causes a stimulus from above" the [cosmic] "other side" above is suppressed as a result. . . .

Thus the Zohar extols the great pleasure that God derives when the "other side" is conquered here below, for then "the glory of God is exalted above all, more than with any other source of praise, and this elevation is greater than any other."

Therefore, a person should not feel dejected, nor should his heart be terribly distressed, even if he is engaged in this conflict all his life. For perhaps it is for this that he was created, and this is his task—constantly to conquer the other side.

WITHIN YOUR REACH

Text 10
IBID., CHAPTER 12

הַמֹּחַ שַׁלִּיט עַל הַלֵּב [כְּמוֹ שֶׁכָּתוּב בַּזֹּהַר פָּרָשַׁת פִּינְחָס]
בְּתוֹלַדְתּוֹ וְטֶבַע יְצִירָתוֹ, שֶׁכָּךְ נוֹצַר הָאָדָם בְּתוֹלַדְתּוֹ, שֶׁכָּל
אָדָם יָכוֹל בִּרְצוֹנוֹ שֶׁבְּמֹחוֹ לְהִתְאַפֵּק וְלִמְשֹׁל בְּרוּחַ תַּאֲוָתוֹ
שֶׁבְּלִבּוֹ, שֶׁלֹּא לְמַלֹּאת מִשְׁאֲלוֹת לִבּוֹ בְּמַעֲשֶׂה דִּבּוּר
וּמַחֲשָׁבָה, וּלְהַסִיחַ דַּעְתּוֹ לְגַמְרֵי מִתַּאֲוַת לִבּוֹ אֶל הַהֵפֶךְ
לְגַמְרֵי.

The brain rules over the heart by virtue of its innately created nature. For the human being was created this way from birth such that, with the power of the will in his mind, he can restrain himself and control the drive of his heart's lust, preventing his heart's desires from finding expression in deed, word and thought. [He can thus] divert his attention completely away from that which his heart craves [and turn his attention] to the exactly opposite direction.

Text 11
DEUTERONOMY 30:14

כִּי קָרוֹב אֵלֶיךָ הַדָּבָר מְאֹד, בְּפִיךָ וּבִלְבָבְךָ לַעֲשׂתוֹ.

It is close to you [i.e., within your reach to] follow the Torah in speech, feeling, and deed.

Question for Discussion

At the start of this lesson, did you view your inner struggles as a Job, a Career, or a Calling? Has your view changed?

Text 12
JAY LITVIN, "SPIRITUAL WARRIOR," CHABAD.ORG

The true warrior longs for the battlefield, for the rest of life seems in comparison like a place where he is able to actualize only a small part of who he is. So he craves the challenge and the encounter. He loves living on the edge. It is here that he is the most of who he is, and where he discovers that he is in fact more than who he thinks he is.

Living as a Jew and a chassid is this experience. It is an encounter with the Almighty and with

JAY LITVIN
1944-2004

Jay Litvin served as medical liaison for Chabad's Children of Chernobyl program, and took a leading role in airlifting children from the areas contaminated by the Chernobyl nuclear disaster; he also founded and directed Chabad's Terror Victims program in Israel.

myself. It is the place of self-discovery and challenge. It requires the bravery of facing who I am and who I am not. It takes a willingness to see the potential of who I can be, and face the smallness of who I have allowed myself to be....

As a spiritual warrior, when I am blessed to be living smack in the middle of the battlefield I am fully alive, wrestling at the edge of who I am. It matters not whether I am in prayer, giving my child a bath, or sitting at my computer. The battlefield includes my personal relationships, my inner desires, my overdrawn bank account, and my constant lack of sleep. It embraces my marriage and employment. My frustration, patience, envy, lust and greed. It is a state of mind, a willingness to find G-d in all places and to meet Him fully, allowing Him to penetrate into the deepest recesses of who I am and to dispel all the images of who I think I am.

Each time, and there are many such times, that I confront the imperative of what I must do with the reluctance of what I want to do; each time that I must transform thoughts and attitudes formed through years of life and conditioning into holy thoughts and holy attitudes, I am on the battlefield....

As a spiritual warrior, I discover my faith when I am at the limits of my faith. I find my love of G-d when I am angry with G-d. I find my trust in the Protector of the world when I am at my most frightened. And I find my obedience to the Almighty when I feel the most rebellious....

The *Tanya* tells us to rejoice when we are challenged within or without, because this is our task: to enter the battlefield. We are, it seems to me, like soldiers who have trained endlessly for battle, and shout in joy when the moment finally arrives to test their abilities and find the real stuff of which they are made.

And this is the spiritual warrior's challenge: to find the stuff of which he is made, whether it is to his liking or not, and bring himself fully into the struggle with himself and his encounter with G-d.

Exercise 3

Think of and write down one inner struggle you currently face that has affected your self-esteem or hampered your motivation to change. How has your view of it changed throughout this lesson?

What is one small step you will take to turn your struggle into an opportunity for growth?

My Personal Take

In the space provided below, write down, in your own words, the two simple truths you learned in today's lesson.

כִּי קָרוֹב אֵלֶיךָ הַדָּבָר מְאֹד, בְּפִיךָ וּבִלְבָבְךָ לַעֲשׂוֹתוֹ. — It is close to you [i.e., within your reach to] follow the Torah in speech, feeling, and deed.

וְהִנֵּה ה' נִצָּב עָלָיו וּמְלֹא כָל הָאָרֶץ כְּבוֹדוֹ, וּמַבִּיט עָלָיו וּבוֹחֵן כְּלָיוֹת וָלֵב, אִם עוֹבְדוֹ כָּרָאוּי. — God stands above you, and [though] the whole earth is full of His glory, He searches your mind and heart to see whether you are serving Him properly.

Key Points

1. Judaism separates these two types of remorse: (1) over a wrong act, and (2) over our character flaw that caused the act. While the former type of remorse is legitimate in the correct context, the latter is not.

2. *Chasidut* teaches us that not only are our internal flaws not valid reasons for despondence, but they are actually sources of joy, and as such, they are the most powerful propellants of growth and refinement.

3. There are two psycho-spiritual prototypes: the "perpetual struggler" and the "perfect person." The vast majority of us are perpetual strugglers; we are engaged in a constant battle with the negative parts of ourselves.

4. The ultimate purpose of creation is this lowly, imperfect world, because it is here that we grapple with darkness, negativity, and coarseness and overcome it, thereby "transforming darkness into light."

5. The perpetual struggler plays a crucial role in this purpose by overcoming the powerful forces of negativity within him- or herself. When we engage and succeed in this inner struggle, we give God immense pleasure.

6. Our struggles should inspire true joy, for overcoming them is a calling that we are privileged by God to fulfill. Furthermore, any unhappiness about our deficiencies implies that we believe we should be "perfect"—which was not God's intention.

7. Our struggles are not just about us and our personal triumphs: every time we overcome a negative impulse within our own heart, the cosmic negativity in the world as a *whole* is suppressed. In short, when

we overcome an individual inner struggle, good triumphs over evil.

8. We cannot control which inner struggles we face; those come from God. If we focus on only the aspects of our struggle we *can* control—our thoughts, speech, and actions—and see these struggles as our Calling in life, rather than as a Job or Career, we are much better poised to overcome the inner battles we face.

Spiritual Warrior

By Jay Litvin

Frankly, I loathe being called a religious person. It sounds so boring.

I'm reminded of a person who once told me how much he envied me. "Life for you is so simple," he said. "Your religion tells you what to do and what not to do, and gives you all the answers."

Boy, I wish.

But, in truth, this is what the word "religion" conjures up: something kind of old and staid, perhaps even a bit crusty. Something calm and peaceful, barely alive and never in motion.

And so, I reject the title of "religious person." I'm just a guy who looks like a religious person.

So then, what am I?

Well, in truth, life feels more to me like a battleground than a prayer service, and my inner reality is more that of a warrior than a pious person.

So, if I have to label myself anything (which I vigorously avoid doing), I would have to call myself a "spiritual warrior." And here's what that means for me.

A warrior is one who enters the battlefield with a healthy dose of fear and a larger dose of love. He fights for a principle, or for his country, or for his king, and his love for these outweighs the fear he feels for his own safety. He requires courage and skill, for he risks his very life.

A warrior loves the battlefield; it is here that he is most alive. He must at all times act with his full awareness and ability; even the slightest lapse will cause his downfall.

The battlefield brings forth from the warrior capabilities and potentials that he didn't even know existed within himself. And so, as he fights, he is in a constant state of self-discovery. The true warrior longs for the battlefield, for the rest of life seems in comparison like a place where he is able to actualize only a small part of who he is. So he craves the challenge and the encounter. He loves living on the edge. It is here that he is the most of who he is, and where he discovers that he is in fact more than who he thinks he is.

Living as a Jew and a chassid is this experience. It is an encounter with the Almighty and with myself. It is the place of self-discovery and challenge. It requires the bravery of facing who I am and who I am not. It takes a willingness to see the potential of who I can be, and face the smallness of who I have allowed myself to be.

When I am living Jewishly, I am living at the edge. I am in a no-man's land where each encounter, each moment, presents an opportunity to learn, to act, to refine and to transform. Sometimes, like King Arthur, I am battling dragons within and without; sometimes I am challenged by beasts that threaten to devour me with their anger and fear; sometimes I am fighting for my own sanity, attempting to reconcile the tactual world with a world which can neither be seen, heard nor touched.

As a spiritual warrior, when I am blessed to be living smack in the middle of the battlefield I am fully alive, wrestling at the edge of who I am. It matters not whether I am in prayer, giving my child a bath, or sitting at my computer. The battlefield includes my personal relationships, my inner desires, my overdrawn bank account, and my constant lack of sleep. It embraces my marriage and employment. My frustration, patience, envy, lust and greed. It is a state of mind, a willingness to find G-d in all places and to meet Him fully, allowing Him to penetrate into the deepest recesses of who I am and to dispel all the images of who I think I am.

Each time, and there are many such times, that I confront the imperative of what I must do with the reluctance of what I want to do; each time that I must transform thoughts and attitudes formed through years of life and conditioning into holy thoughts and holy attitudes, I am on the battlefield. Whether it's giving charity from the few pennies left in the coffer, or taking on an additional responsibility, or offering to help a friend—or not even a friend—when I can barely stay awake, I am on the battlefield. When tragedy strikes my family,

G-d forbid, and I must discover a way to be both genuine with my grief and yet remain cognizant of the good I know that G-d gives to the world, I am being a spiritual warrior.

As a spiritual warrior, I discover my faith when I am at the limits of my faith. I find my love of G-d when I am angry with G-d. I find my trust in the Protector of the world when I am at my most frightened. And I find my obedience to the Almighty when I feel the most rebellious.

I am a spiritual warrior when I fully feel my despair, and find the hope to go on. When I feel betrayed, yet discover my trust. When I reach higher than I should, then fail and fall, only to discover that I have landed at a station higher than the one from which I reached.

On this battlefield called Yiddishkeit, I am stretched to the limit only to find that my limit is nowhere near what I thought it was. I am alive and growing, moving, in process. Scared and exhilarated. Craving victory, and having not the slightest idea of what it means.

To me, all the rest, as Rabbi Schneur Zalman of Liadi says in his *Tanya*, is conceit. To be despondent over the fact that I am constantly in the midst of a struggle is to pretend that I am something more than who I really am. It is to pretend that I am a *tzaddik*, one of the righteous few who have vanquished the negative within themselves, when in fact I can aspire, at my best moments, only to the level of *beinoni*, the spiritual warrior in the battlefield of life. The *Tanya* tells us to rejoice when we are challenged within or without, because this is our task: to enter the battlefield. We are, it seems to me, like soldiers who have trained endlessly for battle, and shout in joy when the moment finally arrives to test their abilities and find the real stuff of which they are made.

And this is the spiritual warrior's challenge: to find the stuff of which he is made, whether it is to his liking or not, and bring himself fully into the struggle with himself and his encounter with G-d.

I find this battle terrifying, because I have no idea where it will lead. It forces me to open myself to G-d and allow Him into the innermost, most intimate confines of myself. It forces me to confront the plaguing question: If I truly let G-d in, what will He do to me once He is there? Who will I be? What will the world have become? And what is my place and purpose within it?

Religious? Me? Hardly. A Torah life is no place for a religious person. Religion is much too safe for such a journey into the unknown, into a meeting place with G-d. Only a warrior can embrace such a task. Only a chassid of the Rebbe can hope to possess such courage.

Spicy Food

By Rabbi Yanki Tauber

One day, about 200 years ago, there was a fire in hell. The whole place burned down. It was bound to happen sooner or later, with those infernal fires burning night and day and the old devils getting careless over the years.

So they called in a troop of architects, contractors and interior designers and built a brand new gehenna. They redid the whole thing, from the landscaping to the ceramic in the bathrooms. But then the righteous folk upstairs in heaven started complaining. "The wicked guys get a new, modern complex, while we're housed in this 5000-year-old dilapidated place? Is this heaven's idea of justice?" It was decided that the righteous were right. The wicked were relocated to the old paradise, which now became the new hell; and the holy folk moved into the old gehenna, which became the new heaven.

Chassidim used to tell this story to illustrate what happened when the founder of Chabad Chassidism, Rabbi Schneur Zalman of Liadi, published his *Tanya* in 1796.

On the cover page of *Tanya*, the author states that he is saying nothing new; all this book is, Rabbi Schneur Zalman insists, is a "collection of sayings" by authors and teachers of Torah of previous generations. Indeed, everything stated in *Tanya* can be found in earlier sources. But as collected and presented by Rabbi Schneur Zalman, they constitute nothing less than a revolutionary understanding of our inner self and our purpose in life.

Before the *Tanya*, the human condition was a spiritual hell. It was a place of dissonance, self-doubt and, above all, a crushing sense of futility over the never-ending conflict between instinct and understanding. Why is it—the typical human asked him-/herself a hundred times a day—that I desire things I don't want to desire? That I need to force myself to do what I've already decided I want to do? That I'm attracted to things that revolt me, and shy away from things I consider good and desirable? Am I such a weak and confused creature that I don't know my own mind and cannot act on my own convictions?

Before the *Tanya*, the typical human being often felt as if there were not one, but two selves residing within his or her body: a lower self that lusts and obsesses and grabs and greeds; and a higher self that commits and shares and is capable of awe and makes space in itself for higher truths. The typical human being yearned for tranquility, for inner quiet, for a resolution of the unending struggle within his fragmented heart. But the yearned-for tranquility never came.

In *Tanya*, Rabbi Schneur Zalman affirmed: yes, there are two selves inside us, and yes, they are engaged in constant battle over control of our lives. We each possess a self-focused "animal soul" which instinctively desires and craves that which preserves, nourishes, enhances and perpetuates itself. And we each have at our core an upward-focused "G-dly soul" that is aware of its source in G-d and strives to reunite with it as a spark craves to be absorbed in the great fire from which it emerged. Our every action, word and thought, our every motive, craving and desire, is an outcome of this ongoing battle within our hearts.

And then Rabbi Schneur Zalman drops his bombshell: this struggle, these conflicting desires, this confusion and self-doubt and inner turmoil, is not a spiritual hell. It is a spiritual heaven.

Indeed, says the *Tanya*, there do exist perfectly righteous individuals—called *tzaddikim*—who have resolved the conflict, whose two souls strive in harmony, whose "selfish" self has been trained and sublimated and brought in sync with their G-dly self. But these individuals are few and far between—a handful in each generation, perhaps a handful in the history of humankind. The rest of us are what Rabbi Schneur Zalman terms *beinonim* ("intermediates")—typical human beings. The rest of us are spiritual warriors, whose calling in life is to fight the battle with integrity, with gusto and with joy.

Why are there *tzaddikin* and *beinonim*? Because G-d desires both:

There are two types of pleasure before G-d. The first is from the complete nullification of evil and its transformation from bitterness to sweetness and from darkness to light by the perfectly righteous. The second [pleasure] is when evil is repelled while it is still at its strongest and mightiest . . . through the efforts of the *beinoni*. . . . As in the analogy of physical food, in which there are two types of delicacies that give pleasure: the first being the pleasure derived from sweet and pleasant foods; and the second, from tart and sour foods, which are spiced and prepared in such a way that they become delicacies that revive the soul . . . (*Tanya*, ch. 27).

If your inner life is tranquil, if no demons plague your thoughts and no dichotomies rend your being, then one of two things are true: either you are a *tzaddik*, or else you are a *beinoni* who abandoned the battlefield. So unless you are so supercilious as to consider yourself a perfectly righteous *tzaddik*, this inner quietude should greatly alarm you. For what meaning, significance and joy can there be in a life that brings no pleasure to G-d?

Once upon a time, there was a heaven and a hell. Then, one day about two hundred years ago, the old heaven became the new hell, and the old hell was refurbished as the new heaven.

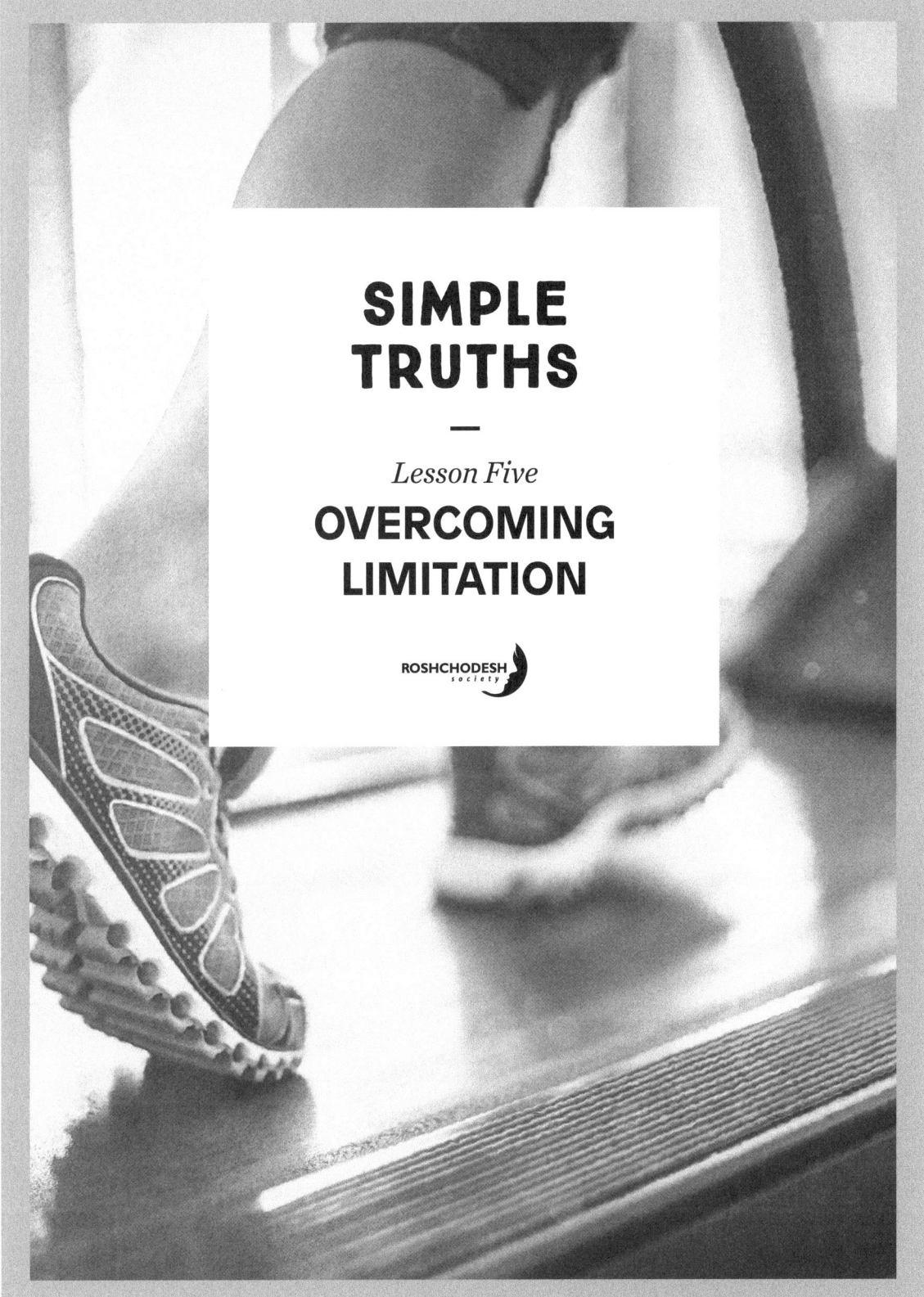

SIMPLE TRUTHS

—

Lesson Five

OVERCOMING LIMITATION

ROSHCHODESH
society

GOOD IS THE ENEMY OF GREAT

Exercise 1

(A) Name three things about yourself that you are proud of:

1

2

3

(B) Name three people you consider to be truly great, and list the qualities and/or achievements for which you admire them.

1

2

3

Question for Discussion

How do you define greatness?

Text 1

JAMES C. COLLINS, *GOOD TO GREAT: WHY SOME COMPANIES MAKE THE LEAP . . . AND OTHERS DON'T* (NEW YORK: HARPERCOLLINS, 2001), P. 1

Good is the enemy of great. And that is one of the key reasons why we have so little that becomes great. We don't have great schools, principally because we have good schools. We don't have great government, principally because we have good government. Few people attain great lives, in large part because it is just so easy to settle for a good life.

JAMES C. COLLINS
1958-

An American business consultant, author, and lecturer on the subject of company sustainability and growth, he has authored or co-authored six books based on his research, including the classic *Built to Last: Successful Habits of Visionary Companies*, a fixture on the *Business Week* best-seller list for more than six years; it has been translated into twenty-five languages. His most recent book is *Great by Choice*.

Questions for Discussion

1. Why do you think people tend not to make the leap from "good" to "great"?

2. Why should people pursue greatness?

3. What do you think compels someone toward greatness?[3]

THE POWER OF JUST ONE MORE

Text 2

SAM PARKER, *212°: THE EXTRA DEGREE* (BEDFORD, TX: WALK THE TALK, 2005), PP. 1–2

At 211 degrees, water is hot. At 212 degrees, it boils. And with boiling water, comes steam. And with steam, you can power a train.

SAM PARKER

Co-founder of InspireYourPeople.com in early 1998, he also has had a sales career in many different industries. Several years ago, he wrote what became an important book to different people and organizations–*212°: The Extra Degree*. His other best sellers include *Lead Simply*, *Smile* and *Move, Cross the Line*, and *Love Your People*.

Text 3

TALMUD, CHAGIGAH 9B

BABYLONIAN TALMUD

A literary work of monumental proportions that draws upon the legal, spiritual, intellectual, ethical, and historical traditions of Judaism. The 37 tractates of the Babylonian Talmud contain the teachings of the Jewish sages from the period after the destruction of the 2nd Temple through the 5th century CE. It has served as the primary vehicle for the transmission of the Oral Law and the education of Jews over the centuries; it is the entry point for all subsequent legal, ethical, and theological Jewish scholarship.

אָמַר לֵיהּ בַּר הֵי הֵי לְהִלֵּל, "מַאי דִכְתִיב, 'וְשַׁבְתֶּם וּרְאִיתֶם בֵּין צַדִּיק לְרָשָׁע, בֵּין עוֹבֵד אֱלֹקִים לַאֲשֶׁר לֹא עֲבָדוֹ' (מַלְאָכִי ג, יח)? הַיְינוּ צַדִּיק הַיְינוּ עוֹבֵד אֱלֹקִים, הַיְינוּ רָשָׁע הַיְינוּ אֲשֶׁר לֹא עֲבָדוֹ?"
אָמַר לֵיהּ, "עֲבָדוֹ וְלֹא עֲבָדוֹ תַּרְוַויְיהוּ צַדִּיקֵי גְמוּרֵי נִינְהוּ. וְאֵינוֹ דוֹמֶה שׁוֹנֶה פִּרְקוֹ מֵאָה פְּעָמִים לְשׁוֹנֶה פִּרְקוֹ מֵאָה וְאֶחָד". אָמַר לֵיהּ, "וּמִשּׁוּם חַד זִמְנָא קָרֵי לֵיהּ לֹא עֲבָדוֹ?"
אָמַר לֵיהּ, "אִין. צֵא וּלְמַד מִשּׁוּק שֶׁל חַמָּרִין, עֲשָׂרָה פַּרְסֵי בְּזוּזָא, חַד עֲשַׂר פַּרְסֵי בִּתְרֵי זוּזֵי".

Bar Hei Hei asked of Hillel: "The verse says, '[In the Messianic era] you will discern between the righteous and the wicked, between the one who serves God and the one who does not serve Him' (Malachi 3:18). Is that not redundant? Is not the righteous person one who serves God and the wicked person one who does not serve Him?"

Hillel replied, "Both the individuals referenced in this verse—'the one who serves' and 'the one who does not serve'—are wholly righteous individuals. Nevertheless, one who reviews his studies only 100 times [is referred to as one who 'does not serve God' because] he cannot be compared to the one who reviews his studies 101 times."

Bar Hei Hei asked, "Because the person reviews his studies one time less, he is considered 'one who does not serve God'?"

"Indeed, that is so," Hillel replied. "Consider, by way of analogy, the market prices for donkey drivers. To hire a donkey driver to travel ten *parsa,* the cost is one *zuz;* whereas for eleven *parsa,* the charge is two *zuz.*"

Text 4

RABBI SHNE'UR ZALMAN OF LIADI, *TANYA*, CH. 15

בִּימֵיהֶם הָיָה הָרְגִילוּת לִשְׁנוֹת כָּל פֶּרֶק מֵאָה פְּעָמִים, כִּדְאִיתָא הָתָם בַּגְּמָרָא מָשָׁל מִשּׁוּק שֶׁל חַמָּרִים שֶׁנִּשְׂכָּרִים לַעֲשָׂר פַּרְסֵי בְּזוּזָא וּלְאַחַד עֲשָׂר פַּרְסֵי בִּתְרֵי זוּזֵי, מִפְּנֵי שֶׁהוּא יוֹתֵר מֵרְגִילוּתָם.

וְלָכֵן זֹאת הַפַּעַם הַמֵּאָה וְאַחַת הַיְתֵרָה עַל הָרְגִילוּת שֶׁהוּרְגַּל מִנְּעוּרָיו שְׁקוּלָה כְּנֶגֶד כֻּלָּן וְעוֹלָה עַל גַּבֵּיהֶן בְּיֶתֶר שְׂאֵת וְיֶתֶר עֹז לִהְיוֹת נִקְרָא עוֹבֵד אֱלֹקִים.

It was standard in that era for scholars to review each lesson 100 times. The Talmud compares [the difference between one who reviews 100 and 101 times] to the [difference in rates at the] donkey-driver market: while the price for a ten-*parsa* hire was one *zuz*, an eleven-*parsa* hire cost two *zuz*, because it exceeded the standard.

The 101st review, which is more than the student's routine, is the equivalent of the previous 100 reviews combined. In fact, it surpasses them, for by its virtue alone this student is considered "one who serves God."

RABBI SHNE'UR ZALMAN OF LIADI (ALTER REBBE)
1745–1812

Chasidic rebbe, halachic authority, and founder of the Chabad movement. The Alter Rebbe was born in Liozna, Belarus, and was among the principal students of the Magid of Mezeritch. His numerous works include the *Tanya*, an early classic containing the fundamentals of Chabad Chasidism, and *Shulchan Aruch HaRav*, an expanded and reworked code of Jewish law.

LEAVING EGYPT

Text 5

RABBI JOSEPH B. SOLOVEITCHIK, *FESTIVAL OF FREEDOM*
(JERSEY CITY, NJ: KTAV PUB. HOUSE, 2006), PP. 60–61

Kabbalistic allegorization . . . sees in every historical occurrence a symbol of a more intimate and personal drama in which man is involved, of a great experience that lies at the very root of one's existential awareness. And so, the story of the exodus is related not only to historical events but to a living reality, as a symbolic narrative of human destiny. In reciting the Haggadah, one is not reminiscing about an ancient past, about people and occurrences enveloped in the mist of the millennia, but rather is telling a personal story, pouring out one's heart, confessing something intense, passionate, and crucial that happened to oneself. At this level, one is preoccupied not with history, but with the living present; not with others, but with oneself and one's own exciting life. . . . A person must see in the story of the exodus, as in a mirror, the inward drama of his or her own soul.

RABBI JOSEPH B. SOLOVEITCHIK
1903–1993

Talmudist and philosopher. A scion of a famous Lithuanian rabbinical family, Rabbi Soloveitchik was one of the most influential Jewish personalities, leaders, and thinkers of the 20th century. In 1941, he became professor of Talmud at RIETS—Yeshiva University; in this capacity, he ordained more rabbis than anyone else in Jewish history. Among his published works are *Halakhic Man* and *Lonely Man of Faith*.

Text 6

MISHNAH, PESACHIM 10:5

בְּכָל דּוֹר וָדוֹר חַיָּיב אָדָם לִרְאוֹת אֶת עַצְמוֹ כְּאִילוּ הוּא יָצָא מִמִּצְרָיִם.

In every generation, we must view ourselves as if we, too, left Egypt.

MISHNAH

The first authoritative work of Jewish law that was codified in writing. The Mishnah contains the oral traditions that were passed down from teacher to student; it supplements, clarifies, and systematizes the commandments of the Torah. Due to the continual persecution of the Jewish people, it became increasingly difficult to guarantee that these traditions would not be forgotten. Rabbi Yehudah Hanasi therefore redacted the Mishnah at the end of the 2nd century. It serves as the foundation for the Talmud.

Question for Discussion

How might our ancestors' slavery and their journey to freedom reflect the narrative of our own lives?

Text 7

ADAPTED FROM THE REBBE, RABBI MENACHEM M.
SCHNEERSON, *LIKUTEI SICHOT*, VOLUME 2, P. 348

Mitzrayim, the Hebrew word for "Egypt," means "borders" and "narrows." On the spiritual level, the journey from Egypt is a journey from the boundaries that limit us—an exodus from the narrow straits of habit, convention, and ego to the "good, broad land" of the infinite potential of our Godly soul.

And the journey from *Mitzrayim* is a perpetual one: what is expansive and uninhibited by yesterday's standards, is narrow and confining in light of the added wisdom and new possibilities of today's station. Thus, each of life's "journeys" is an exodus from the land of *Mitzrayim*: having transcended yesterday's limitations, we must again journey from the *Mitzrayim* that our present norm represents, relative to our newly uncovered potential.

RABBI MENACHEM MENDEL SCHNEERSON
1902–1994

The towering Jewish leader of the 20th century, known as "the Lubavitcher Rebbe," or simply as "the Rebbe." Born in southern Ukraine, the Rebbe escaped Nazi-occupied Europe, arriving in the U.S. in June 1941. The Rebbe inspired and guided the revival of traditional Judaism after the European devastation, impacting virtually every Jewish community the world over. The Rebbe often emphasized that the performance of just one additional good deed could usher in the era of Mashiach. The Rebbe's scholarly talks and writings have been printed in more than 200 volumes.

Text 8

RABBI ADIN EVEN-ISRAEL (STEINSALTZ), FROM AN ADDRESS ON JUNE 17, 2004 AT A GATHERING MARKING THE TENTH *YAHRTZEIT* OF THE LUBAVITCHER REBBE, IN THE JFK LIBRARY, BOSTON, MA

The most remarkable thing about the Rebbe—and this is something you could see in everything he did, in virtually every sentence he spoke or wrote—was his enormous drive to always supersede oneself, to always do more. . . .

More than twelve years ago, I wrote a letter to the Rebbe. I tried to describe what I was doing, tried to explain that one of the projects I'm involved with is enough work to occupy me all day, every day. There was also a second project, which was also enough work to fill my entire day. And then there was a third undertaking which was a full day's work. I told the Rebbe that I find it hard to carry on with them all, and that every day is more difficult than the one before, because there is just so much. So [I asked the Rebbe,] what should my priorities be? What should I cut out? . . . He responded . . . "continue all the things that you are doing, and add more to all of them."

You know the famous story about the farmer who comes to the rabbi complaining about his small house so full of children, it's unbearable? So the rabbi tells him to take a goat into his house, a noisy, smelly, dirty goat. Very soon the farmer comes back to the rabbi. "Every problem I had is worse!" he cries. The rabbi tells him to take the goat out. So he takes the goat out of his house, and soon he's back to tell the rabbi what a big, wonderful house he now has! . . .

RABBI ADIN EVEN-ISRAEL (STEINSALTZ)
1937–

Talmudist, author, and philosopher. Rabbi Even-Israel Steinsaltz is considered one of the foremost Jewish thinkers of the 20th century. Praised by *Time* magazine as a "once-in-a-millennium scholar," he has been awarded the Israel Prize for his contributions to Jewish study. He lives in Jerusalem and is the founder of the Israel Institute for Talmudic Publications, a society dedicated to the translation and elucidation of the Talmud.

What the Rebbe did was similar, and yet quite different. When people complained about how hard their work was, he would give them more to do. When they complained how [difficult] *that* was, he would suggest [that they] take on something more. . . .

Obviously, this is against the laws of nature . . . we are confined by the limits of the human condition. How could [the Rebbe] overburden people like this? I will give an answer from the realm of physics: You [can] have a certain amount of pressure on something, and there is a point at which it can take no more. [But] when you put ten times [or] one hundred times *that* pressure on it, something happens. The molecules collapse, and the very nature of the object changes. . . .

This was what the Rebbe wanted to do. He wanted to change the very nature of human matter, human behavior, the very way the human being operates. With every person he encountered, he tried to change their nature into something completely different.

Exercise 2

Describe a time in your life when you pushed yourself beyond the limits of what you believed was possible. What was the result?

FOR A PURPOSE
BEYOND OURSELVES

Question for Discussion

The following list contains some of the most famous Nobel Prize winners and the reason for which they received arguably the world's most prestigious prize. What is/are the common denominator(s) among them?

Figure 5.1

Nobel Prize Winners

Marie Curie
Physics Prize 1903, 1911

Extraordinary service rendered by her research on the radiation phenomena (Radioactive compounds became important also in the field of medicine, where they are used to treat tumors.)

Albert Einstein
Physics Prize 1921

Service to Theoretical Physics, and especially the discovery of the law of the photoelectric effect

Ernest Hemingway
Literature Prize 1954

A nonviolent campaign against racism in the United States

Martin Luther King Jr.
Peace Prize 1964

Mastery of the art of narrative and for the great influence he exerted on contemporary style

Nelson Mandela and Frederik Willem de Klerk
Peace Prize 1993

Work for the peaceful termination of the apartheid regime, and for laying the foundations for a new democratic South Africa

Elie Wiesel
Peace Prize 1986

A lifetime of work to bear witness to the Nazi genocide, and fighting indifference and the attitude that "it's no concern of mine"

FINDING GREATNESS

Text 9

TALMUD, MEGILAH 6B

אִם יֹאמַר לְךָ אָדָם יָגַעְתִּי וְלֹא מָצָאתִי—אַל תַּאֲמֵן.

לֹא יָגַעְתִּי וּמָצָאתִי—אַל תַּאֲמֵן.

יָגַעְתִּי וּמָצָאתִי—תַּאֲמֵן.

If someone says, "I have worked hard but I have not found [success]," don't believe him;

"I have not worked hard and I have found [success]," don't believe him;

"I have worked hard and I have found [success]," believe him!

Text 10

THE REBBE, RABBI MENACHEM M. SCHNEERSON,
TORAT MENACHEM 5743, 3:1238–1239

כַּאֲשֶׁר יְהוּדִי מִתְנַהֵג, בְּתוֹקֶף הַמָּלֵא שֶׁל "כָּל עַצְמוֹתַי
תֹּאמַרְנָה" יַחַד עִם הַהִתְבַּטְּלוּת הַמְּלֵאָה וְהַבִּיצוּעַ הַמָּלֵא שֶׁל
שְׁלִיחוּתוֹ הָאֱלֹקִית בְּחַיֵּי יוֹם-יוֹם שֶׁלּוֹ, יֵשׁ לוֹ הַצְלָחָה בִּלְתִּי
רְגִילָה, יְתֵירָה לְאֵין-עֲרוֹךְ מִמִּדַּת הֶעָמָל וְהַיְגִיעָה שֶׁהִשְׁקִיעַ
בְּדָבָר, כְּפִי שֶׁחֲכָמֵינוּ ז"ל מְבַטְּאִים זֹאת בְּמַאֲמָר הַקָּצָר "יָגַעְתָּ
- וּמָצָאתָ", הַהַצְלָחָה מִן הַיְגִיעָה הִיא בְּאוֹפֶן שֶׁל "מְצִיאָה",
דָּבָר יָקָר שֶׁנִּמְצָא, לְמָשָׁל, בָּרְחוֹב, שֶׁעֶרְךְ הַדָּבָר גָּדוֹל לְאֵין-
עֲרוֹךְ וְלֹלֹא יַחַס לְגַבֵּי הֶעָמָל שֶׁל הַהִתְכּוֹפְפוּת וַהֲרָמַת הַדָּבָר
וַהֲבָאָתוֹ לִרְשׁוּתוֹ.

הַהַצְלָחָה עַל-טִבְעִית זוּ קְשׁוּרָה בִּמְיוּחָד עִם חוֹדֶשׁ נִיסָן, מִשּׁוּם
שֶׁבְּחוֹדֶשׁ זֶה הִנְהִיג הַקָּבָּ"ה הַנְהָגָה נִיסִּית, בְּהוֹצִיאוֹ אֶת עַם
יִשְׂרָאֵל, אֶת כָּל הַיְהוּדִים, מִגָּלוּת מִצְרַיִם, וְהִבְטִיחַ שֶׁכַּאֲשֶׁר
יְהוּדִי יְקַבֵּל עַל עַצְמוֹ הַחְלָטוֹת לְבַצֵּעַ "יְצִיאַת מִצְרַיִם" עִם
עַצְמוֹ וְעִם סְבִיבָתוֹ, מְסַיֵּיעַ לוֹ הַקָּבָּ"ה לְמַעֲלָה מִדֶּרֶךְ הַטֶּבַע.

When a Jew lives his daily life with the utmost effort and single-minded dedication to his Divine purpose in the world, he is blessed with extraordinary success, greater than the effort he put in, like our sages taught in the short maxim, "if you put in effort you will *find*." The success comes in the way of a "finding," like a precious item that you happened upon in the street that is worth so much more than the effort you put in to simply pick it up and take it home.

This supernatural sort of success is especially connected with the month of *Nisan*, the month in which God miraculously redeemed the Jews from their bondage in Egypt. When a Jew resolves to leave his personal Egypt, he taps into

this supernatural energy and receives supernatural Divine assistance.

Exercise 3

Go back to the three things about yourself that
you said you were proud of in the beginning of this
lesson. Choose one of them. How will you take it
from "good" to "great"—specifically, by (1) going
beyond your norm, and (2) by doing so in the fulfillment of a purpose greater than yourself?

My Personal Take

In the space provided below, write down, in your own words, the two simple truths you learned in today's lesson.

בְּכָל דּוֹר וָדוֹר חַיָּב | In every generation
אָדָם לִרְאוֹת אֶת | every person must see
עַצְמוֹ כְּאִלּוּ הוּא | oneself as if he or she had
יָצָא מִמִּצְרַיִם. | personally left Egypt.

יָגַעְתִּי וְלֹא | If someone says, "I worked hard, yet
מָצָאתִי – אַל | I have not succeeded," don't believe
תַּאֲמִין. לֹא | this person. If someone says, "I have
יָגַעְתִּי וּמָצָאתִי | not worked hard, yet I have succeed-
– אַל תַּאֲמִין. | ed," don't believe this person. If some-
יָגַעְתִּי וּמָצָאתִי | one says, "I have worked hard, and I
תַּאֲמִין. – | have succeeded," believe this person.

Key Points

1. Greatness is not about a certain threshold or achievement, or even about reaching a certain measure of self-perfection. Rather, greatness is measured by the extent to which we exert ourselves beyond our perceived limitations.

2. Going beyond our perceived limitations means freeing ourselves from that which personally enslaves us—our negative tendencies, our bad habits, our narrow perspectives, our egos, as well as the things about us that are perfectly "good," but simply stagnant, stuck, or not in a process of growth. This is the deeper meaning of "leaving Egypt."

3. Greatness is also not measured by personal gain or benefit, but by transcending one's own desires in order to focus on a greater cause or purpose, leaving a legacy that transcends all self-benefit or self-accomplishment.

4. When we put in the grueling effort that it takes to rise above our nature, with the purpose of fulfilling our divine mission, God rewards us with success that is, similarly, boundless—above and beyond our wildest expectations.

5. This success that God grants us is not just a response to our toil, but a natural result; when we put in the extraordinary effort it takes to transcend the narrowness and smallness of self-centeredness, *that* is the measure of true greatness.

APPENDIX

THE REBBE, RABBI MENACHEM M. SCHNEERSON,
TORAT MENACHEM 5751, 4:159

כַּיָּדוּעַ שֶׁהַכַּוָּונָה וְתַכְלִית דְּבְרִיאַת הָאָדָם וִירִידַת הַנְּשָׁמָה
לְמַטָּה וּשְׁלֵימוּת (תַּעֲנוּג) הָאָדָם כְּפִי שֶׁנִּקְבַּע עַל יְדֵי הַקָּדוֹשׁ
בָּרוּךְ הוּא, שֶׁמַּה שֶׁמְּקַבֵּל לֹא יְהְיֶה "נַהֲמָא דְכִיסוּפָא"...,
אֶלָּא שֶׁיִּתְיַיגֵּעַ בָּזֶה עַל יְדֵי עֲבוֹדָתוֹ בְּעַצְמוֹ, וּבִלְשׁוֹן חַז"ל—
"לֹא יָגַעְתִּי וּמָצָאתִי אַל תַּאֲמִין, יָגַעְתִּי וּמָצָאתִי תַּאֲמִין",
[וּבְפַשְׁטוּת — כֵּן הוּא טֶבַע כָּל בְּנֵי אָדָם (אֲפִילוּ שֶׁאֵינָם־
יְהוּדִים), וְעַל אַחַת כַּמָּה וְכַמָּה בְּנֵי יִשְׂרָאֵל, וְעַל אַחַת כַּמָּה
וְכַמָּה כַּאֲשֶׁר הֵם עוֹשִׂים עֲבוֹדָתָם בִּיגִיעָה יְתֵירָה לְמַעְלָה
מִדֶּרֶךְ הַטֶּבַע וְהָרְגִילוּת שֶׁלָּהֶם (בִּבְחִינַת "עוֹבֵד אֱלֹקִים").]]

Essential to the fulfillment of the purpose of the creation of the human being and the descent of the divine soul into the world, as established by God—and also essential for a person's ability to reach completion and a sense of gratification—is that the human being should not be the recipient of "bread of shame" [i.e., an unearned "free lunch," in which he cannot take pride]. Rather, we must toil and work in order to achieve and succeed. As our sages say, "Do not believe one who says, 'I have not toiled and yet I have succeeded,' but believe one who says, 'I have toiled and I have succeeded.' This notion [that only toil breeds success] is a rule of human nature, and is especially true when people work in a manner that defies their natural tendencies and habits, in the manner of the "one who serves God."

Leaving Egypt for Good: The Inner Power of Passover

By Shifra Hendrie

"As in the days when you left Egypt, I will show you wonders" Micah 7:15.

On the fifteenth of the Hebrew month of Nissan, Jews around the world will sit together with family and friends. They will sit at tables covered with white cloths, illuminated with candlelight, sparkling with silver, china and crystal. Throughout the night, they will taste the richness of wine, the bitterness of horseradish, and the subtle pure taste of matzah, the bread of faith.

On the seder night, we celebrate our liberation from slavery in Egypt, our redemption and freedom.

And yet, we are still waiting to be free.

When I was a small child, I lived in Chicago. We weren't observant, but my grandparents were. And every Passover (Pesach), we would go to their apartment—my parents, my brothers and I—together with all my aunts, uncles and cousins, to celebrate the seder.

I remember my Uncle Artie and my Aunt Shiffy joking, the kids clowning around, my grandfather talking about the Exodus from Egypt and my grandmother saying: "Samuel, I'm hungry! Can you please hurry so we can eat?"

I never wanted my grandfather to hurry. I would have loved it if he had told the story of the Exodus all night long. Because from as far back as I can remember, at the seder—in the eating, the drinking and the telling of the story—I could feel the walls of the world shifting, opening and moving back. I could feel the presence of something else; something sparkling, something powerful, profoundly in motion, real and alive.

Many years have passed since my grandparents passed away. There were years—lots of years—when I didn't go to any seder. There were years when I didn't even know that Pesach had come and gone.

Then began my own journey back—back to my roots, to the roots of my grandparents and great-grandparents, to the roots of all the generations that came before. My journey brought me all the way back to the generation of the Exodus from Egypt, an Exodus which is still occurring today.

The slavery of Egypt was the most profound and all-encompassing that ever existed, as it was not only physical but spiritual as well. The redemption from Egypt took place in the midst of thunderous miracles, and through it, both bodies and souls become free.

But that freedom did not last. True, the Exodus was the prototype for every redemption that would ever follow. It was a world-altering event that led to the birth of the Jewish nation and the giving of the Torah, the Divine mandate for all of humanity. But it was incomplete.

G-d took us out of Egypt, but He did not take Egypt out of us.

Kabbalah explains that the Hebrew word for Egypt, *Mitzrayim*, means limitations, boundaries, constraints. In breaking out of Egypt, we were freed from those constraints, changed forever. From the moment Pharaoh let us go, there was no longer any force in the world powerful enough to keep a Jew from connecting with G-d. No force in the world.

But inside the Jew—that's a different story. Many times over the millennia of our history we were enslaved, oppressed, expelled—and much worse. The world has not been a hospitable place for the Jews. But in each of those situations, Jews kept the Torah. Though the world has tried to destroy the Jewish nation time and time again, the Jews have never agreed to disappear.

Nevertheless, Egypt remains alive inside the hearts of each one of us. It makes us feel small and unworthy. It makes us forget who we are and who we could become. It makes us believe that we have to blend in with those who seem bigger and more powerful than ourselves. It gives us the stubborn illusion that the world is solid and real, and that the intimate presence of G-d and our own souls is a fantasy or a dream. This "slave mentality" is the cause of all the limiting beliefs, uncertainties and fears that are in our way. It makes us feel helpless and disempowered. It cuts us off from the miracles of our past, the potential of our future and our own truly infinite power to change our world for good.

It all comes down to this: Until we free ourselves from the inner Egypt we will never be truly free.

But once we do, we will never be slaves again—to anything, or anyone. Not even ourselves.

The generation that left Egypt ran up against the same basic problem again and again. They were conditioned to think like slaves. They feared the power of the nations who opposed them, and they could not fully internalize —trust and rely upon—their relationship with G-d.

But Kabbalah tells us a fascinating thing. It says that the souls of the generation that left Egypt will be reincarnated in our times, in the generation of the final redemption. It is the task of this generation to finally transform the inner Egypt and set ourselves and all our descendants free.

Passover occurs in the month of Nissan. Nissan is called the Rosh Hashanah, the New Year, of redemption. The name Nissan itself contains within it the Hebrew word for miracle (nes). And each Nissan, as it enters, brings with it exactly that—a vast potential for miracles of redemption, a new level of potential that was never present in the world before.

You might sense this; you might not. But either way, it doesn't change the facts. As the last generation of exile and the first of redemption, we were born with the slave mentality, but only in order that we can transform it once and for all. We are meant to come face-to-face with those feelings of smallness and helplessness, the fears and uncertainties, and the fact that the constraints and challenges of our physical world still seem all too real. But only so that we can finally leave them behind.

You have to feel these things, true. But you don't have to believe in them. You don't have to let them control your life anymore.

According to the Lubavitcher Rebbe, at this crucial and transitional time in history we can and must begin to use our new potential—our miraculous potential—in every aspect of our lives. It's not enough to simply stop being slaves, to become a nation among nations. We must go much higher than that. Each one of us, through the intimacy and intensity of our connection with G-d, now has the power to connect with our own concealed essence as well. From that place, we become true partners in Creation. Not only will our lives become miraculous, but miracles will become a part of our very nature.

Here's a little secret that will help. The truth is that everything is already a miracle. Since G-d is bringing this world into existence from divine "nothingness" at every moment, everything is intentional, everything is miraculous and everything is an alive, moving expression of its infinite Source. But this reality can't just remain an idea. It must be internalized; become a part of our daily consciousness, our ordinary lives.

So let's start with you.

What would change in your life if you connected to this reality and began to tap into a still-unexplored level of awareness and power? Would you notice the myriad and continuous expressions of Divine Providence in your life and world? Would you feel more connected and empowered? Bolder, more confident, less afraid?

What would your relationships be like? What would you be committed to? What would you create?

You don't have to wait. In fact, waiting is the last thing you should do.

This Nissan, it's time to approach each challenge and every opportunity of your life with a new belief, the belief that it is now within your nature to make miracles, to create redemption. This belief—and the actions that go with it—will change your world.

We don't have to wait for next year in Jerusalem. As we sit by the seder table this year, may we be truly free!

The Reinvention of Man

By Rabbi Adin Even-Israel (Steinsaltz)

From an address delivered by Rabbi Steinsaltz on June 17, 2004, at a gathering marking the 10th yahrtzeit *of the Lubavitcher Rebbe, Rabbi Menachem M. Schneerson, in the JFK Library in Boston, Mass.*

The Talmud, in a few short sentences, records a dispute that took place some 2000 years ago between the two major ideological and halachic schools of the time, *Beit Shammai* ("House of Shammai") and *Beit Hillel* ("House of Hillel"). The subject of their dispute was: "Is it better for a man to be born or not to be born?" For two and a half years they argued. When the decision finally came, it was agreed by all that it's more worthwhile to not be born. The only qualifier was that once one is born, one should at least do the best one can.

There are hundreds of debates between Beit Shammai and Beit Hillel recorded in the Talmud, and most of them concern questions of Torah law and ritual, such as, when sitting down to the Shabbat meal, do we first recite the kiddush, or do we first wash our hands? To find a dispute over whether or not the existence of man is worthwhile among the other disputes seems strange. What's the basis of their disagreement?

If one wishes make a general summary of the difference between the two schools, it would be this: Beit Shammai were idealists while Beit Hillel were realists. Beit Shammai were thinking about a perfect picture, an ideal existence; Beit Hillel thought of existence as it is. This is, of course, a gross simplification, but it is a common thread in their debates. Beit Shammai were people of the heaven. Anything they see in this world, they don't want to see its limits; they want to see it in its totality, in its ultimate significance. Beit Hillel constrain themselves to problems and situations of our lives as they are. This makes for many differences in many questions.

In our times, in this world, we rule according to Beit Hillel. And in Moshiach's times, the law will reverse itself and we will rule according to Beit Shammai. In an imperfect world law will follow Beit Hillel and in an ideal world it can follow perfection and rule according to Beit Shammai.

So it all depends on what is your view of the world, what view of existence you have before you, how you perceive the question of "what is man?" Beit Hillel says that in imperfection we should deal with what we have. That it's really a question of "how to be." Beit Shammai says that we cannot disregard the big theoretical picture. It's not enough to simply do what you have to do -- it has to add up to something in the big picture.

In many ways, man is a creation that doesn't justify the effort put into it. In real life people sin, they don't care. Beit Hillel tried to maintain a positive outlook and say: we're here, we try to do things. Beit Shammai, however, insisted on perceiving man compared with what he could be, compared with angels. Seen in this light, there are just too many imperfections. In the words of Psalms 8:5, *Mah enush kee tizkerenu*, "What is man, that You are mindful of him?"

The most remarkable thing about the Rebbe—and this is something you could see in everything he did, you could hear this in snippets of his discussions with people, in virtually every sentence he spoke or wrote—was his enormous drive. To always supersede oneself, to always do more.

I experienced this myself in my relationship with the Rebbe. I know that one shouldn't speak of oneself, but what can I do, this is a subject I know a little bit about. . . . More than twelve years ago, I wrote a letter to the Rebbe. I tried to describe what I was doing, tried to explain that one project I'm involved with is enough work to occupy me all day, every day. There was also a second project, which was also enough work to fill my entire day. And then there was a third undertaking which was a full day's work. I told the Rebbe that I find it hard to carry on with them all, and that every day is more difficult than the one before, because there is just so much. So what should my priorities be? What should I cut out? This is the letter I wrote. So he responded—this is practically the last letter I received from the Rebbe—the Rebbe's answer was, "continue all these things that you are doing and add more to all of them." He demanded these things. How can I explain? You know the famous story about the farmer who comes to the rabbi complaining about his small house so full of children. It's unbearable. So the rabbi tells him to take a goat into his house, a noisy, smelly, dirty goat. Very soon the farmer comes back to the rabbi. "Every problem I had is worse!" he cries. The rabbi tells him to take the goat out. So he takes the goat out of his house and soon he's back to tell the rabbi what a big wonderful house he now has. A very old story but what the Rebbe did was similar and yet quite different. When people complained about how hard their work was he would give them more to do. When they complained how terrible *that* was he would give them even more. He told them to add the goat, and then he'd give them camels to put in their house! That was the way he worked all the time. Whenever anybody complained about their inability to cope or the hard times they endured, he would suggest "take on something more."

Obviously, this is against the laws of nature. You have a certain amount of space, you are confined by the limits of the human condition. What did the Rebbe do? How could he overburden people like this? I will give an answer from the realm of physics. Once, when I was a nice, honest, young man I was interested in that field. There is something in physics -- you have a certain amount of pressure on something, and there is a point at which it can take no more. When you put ten times, one hundred times that pressure on it, something happens. The molecules collapse and the very nature of the object changes. In astronomy you have what is called "white dwarves." These are small stars, the size of the earth, sometimes even smaller. The mass they contain is many times that of the sun. Each cubic centimeter weighs many tons. Why? Because the matter collapsed and

became something else, the laws themselves changed.

In a way, this was what the Rebbe wanted to do. He wanted to change the very nature of human matter, human behavior, the very way the human being operates. With everybody he encountered, he tried to change their nature into something completely different. They weren't people anymore, they are something else.

The first person that the Rebbe tried this experiment on was himself. There are letters he wrote back in 1950, when Chassidim pushed him to become rebbe. They are unusual for him, very emotional: "How can I take this suffering? I didn't deserve it. I don't want it. It's not me." He writes that he is "not able to, not willing" to take on the position. He says, "They tear the flesh from my bones when they ask me to be the rebbe." If he would have been asked "to be or not to be?" his answer would have been, as Beit Shammai, "Not to be." But then he did it. He undertook to become something he had insisted he was not. To become something that goes beyond being a human being.

Which brings us back to the Talmud's question. After two-and-a-half years of debate, *all* the sages, both the optimists and the pessimists, had to admit that man was a failed experiment. The only thing that could be said was, "now that we're here, let's do the best we can." But there is a different way of answering the question. Instead of answering "yes" or "no", to find a third answer. This is what the Rebbe tried to do. He said, instead of answering the question "is man worthy of being here in this universe?" let us make a new human being, a new kind of existence from which the answer must be positive.

Increasingly through the years the Rebbe's emphasis was on Moshiach. He spoke of the Moshiach again and again and again. He made it clear in his first public speech that this is the matter that he was interested in. He expressed the same notion thousands of times; in everything he said there was always the same idea—that Moshiach is coming.

Now, Moshiach is not a small little thing that happens from time to time. Moshiach is really and truly the end of history. Moshiach means there will be a time that not only will things be slightly better, they will be as they should be. It means all the things we have tried in all the generations, in all the ages, will be fulfilled. The way things were up until now, we advance in certain ways, and then we have a failure, a backlash. This is what history is made of. The story of the attempts and failures of humanity. Moshiach means a time will come that problems will be solved. That from that time on there will no longer be a matter of failing. The end of time, "the end of days" in biblical terminology. The end of the ups and downs of human history in creating something that is completely new, completely different. Bringing Moshiach is much harder than creating a state of Israel or creating a United States of America. Bringing Moshiach is changing the world in a way that never reverts back. Instead of all this erratic movement of existence, where every ascent is followed by failure, the Rebbe aimed higher by asking people to do what they cannot do. What's called in Chassidic thought "b'chol m'odecha." This phrase appears in the Shema and is commonly translated "with all your might" but really means "with all your more." It means giving your life and everything that you possess, and then you give more. What is the more? The things that you cannot do. This was the Rebbe's approach: put so much work on a person until he becomes something else. The Rebbe was not interested in creating a crop of "outreach professionals"; he wanted to make every home into a "Chabad House." He wanted to literally change people, their very nature. He kept on asking for more, demanding more, never satisfied because we still didn't get to a different plane of existence, to the collapse of matter as it were, the collapse of the existing structure and the building of a very different structure of reality. More compact, less empty, better. Not simply changing a few people here and there—this is a reality that comes of something that must be done by everybody. When in his last years the Rebbe cried that we must bring Moshiach now, he pushed harder, again and again.

What he was speaking of were things that we cannot do, things that are impossible, thing that we could never complete in just a lifetime. Because it is said that when Moshiach comes when we pass into the world of impossibilities, when we achieve not only what we can do but also what we cannot do. . . .

The Rebbe wanted to do something that was more far reaching than any revolution. He wanted to make this kind of irreversible change in human nature, this change in human history, he wanted it to become entirely different.

The Rebbe understood people, he understood them very well because many of them revealed themselves, became more than naked in his presence. They told everything that they had to tell, their failings, their weaknesses. And his message to us was: *Run! And if you cannot run—Walk! And if you cannot walk—Crawl! But always advance, advance, advance!*

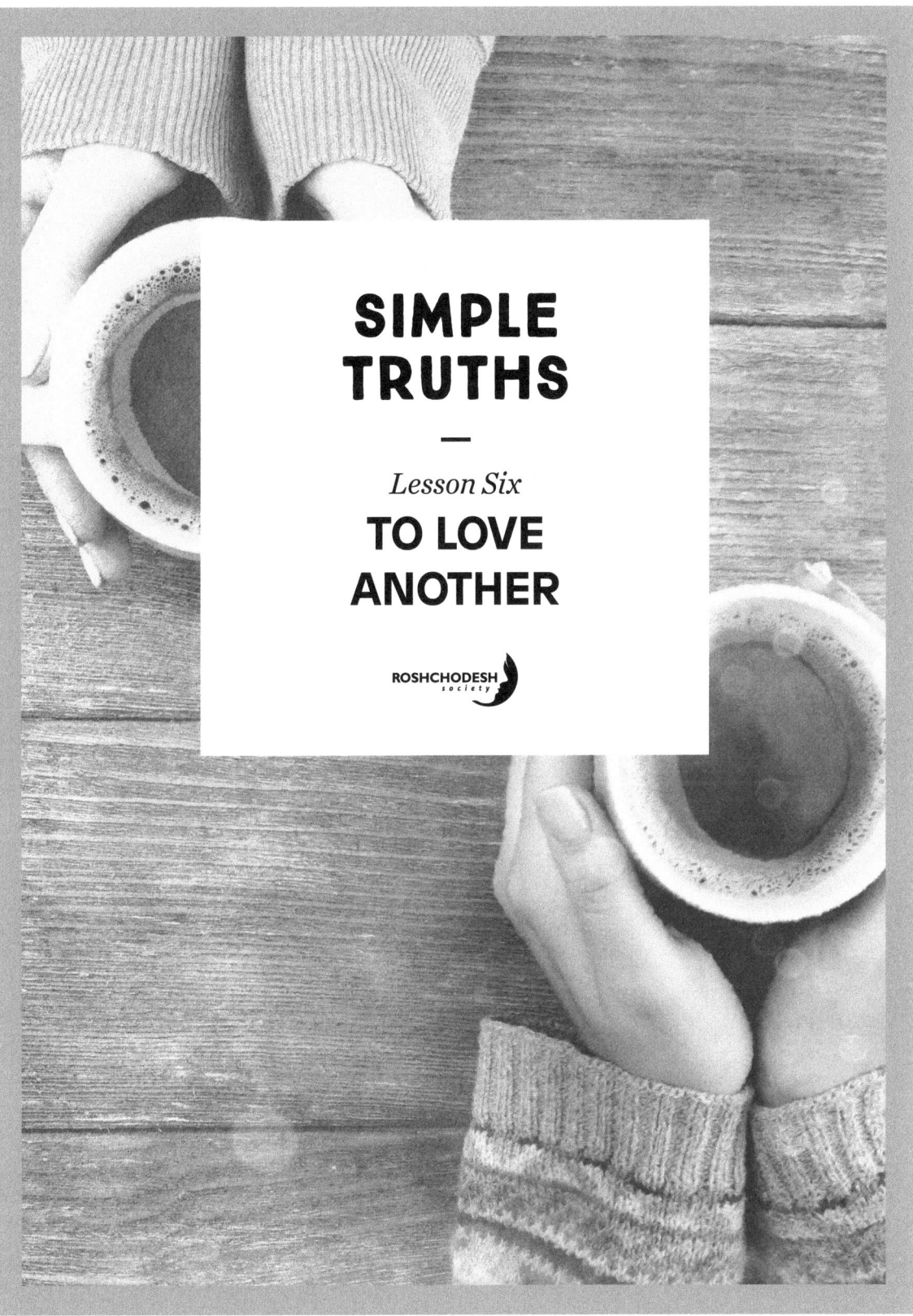

SIMPLE TRUTHS

—

Lesson Six

TO LOVE ANOTHER

ROSHCHODESH
society

INTRODUCTION—
STUCK IN AN ELEVATOR

Figure 6.1

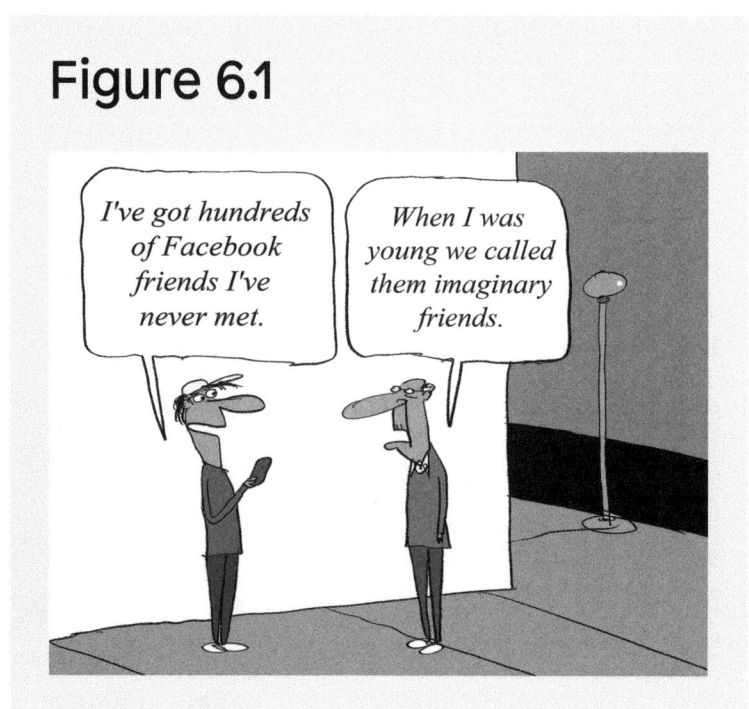

Question for Discussion

Four people are riding in an elevator:

- An inner-city-hardened teenager;

- A suburban soccer mom;

- A distinguished university professor; and

- A guitar-strapping, marijuana-smoking hippie.

Suddenly, the elevator screeches to a halt, suspended between floors. It takes firefighters four hours to extricate them. To make matters worse, they have no cell phone signal or Wi-Fi access. What is likely to transpire during those four hours?

LOVE YOUR FELLOW—THE BASIS OF TORAH

Text 1

SIFRA, LEVITICUS 19:18

וְאָהַבְתָּ לְרֵעֲךָ כָּמוֹךָ – רַבִּי עֲקִיבָא אוֹמֵר, זֶה כְּלָל גָּדוֹל בַּתּוֹרָה.

"Love your fellow as yourself" (Leviticus 19:18). Rabbi Akiva said, "This is a great principle in the Torah."

SIFRA (*TORAT KOHANIM*)

An ancient rabbinic exegesis on the Book of Leviticus. The subject matter of this work is predominately Temple-era-related laws inasmuch as much of the Book of Leviticus focuses on the Temple service. According to Maimonides, the compiler and editor of this work was the Talmudic sage Rav (175–247 CE). Others attribute it to an earlier redactor. The work is quoted often in the Talmud.

Text 2

TALMUD, SHABBAT 31A

בָּא לִפְנֵי הִלֵּל, גַּיְירֵיהּ. אָמַר לֵיהּ: "דַּעֲלָךְ סְנֵי לְחַבְרָךְ לָא תְּעֲבֵיד. זוֹ הִיא כָּל הַתּוֹרָה כּוּלָהּ וְאִידָךְ פֵּירוּשָׁה הוּא, זִיל גְּמוֹר."

The Gentile approached Hillel, who converted him, and told him: "What is hateful to you, do not do to your fellow. This is all of Torah in its entirety; the rest is commentary. Go and learn it!"

BABYLONIAN TALMUD

A literary work of monumental proportions that draws upon the legal, spiritual, intellectual, ethical, and historical traditions of Judaism. The 37 tractates of the Babylonian Talmud contain the teachings of the Jewish sages from the period after the destruction of the 2nd Temple through the 5th century CE. It has served as the primary vehicle for the transmission of the Oral Law and the education of Jews over the centuries; it is the entry point for all subsequent legal, ethical, and theological Jewish scholarship.

Text 3

NACHMANIDES, LEVITICUS 19:18

וְטַעַם "וְאָהַבְתָּ לְרֵעֲךָ כָּמוֹךָ" הַפְלָגָה, כִּי לֹא יְקַבֵּל לֵב הָאָדָם שֶׁיֶּאֱהֹב אֶת חֲבֵרוֹ כְּאַהֲבָתוֹ אֶת נַפְשׁוֹ.

"Love your fellow as yourself" is a hyperbolic statement. The human heart cannot love another as it loves itself.

RABBI MOSHE BEN NACHMAN (NACHMANIDES, RAMBAN)
1194–1270

Scholar, philosopher, author and physician. Nachmanides was born in Spain and served as leader of Iberian Jewry. In 1263, he was summoned by King James of Aragon to a public disputation with Pablo Cristiani, a Jewish apostate. Though Nachmanides was the clear victor of the debate, he had to flee Spain because of the resulting persecution. He moved to Israel and helped reestablish communal life in Jerusalem. He authored a classic commentary on the Pentateuch and a commentary on the Talmud.

Text 4

RABBI YEHUDAH BEN ELIEZER OF TROYES, *MINCHAT YEHUDAH*, AD LOC.

יִתְנַהֵג אָדָם עִם חֲבֵרוֹ בְּאַהֲבָה. מַה שֶּׁלֹּא יִרְצֶה שֶׁיַּעֲשׂוּ לוֹ, אַל יַעֲשֵׂהוּ לַחֲבֵרוֹ, וְזֶהוּ "וְאָהַבְתָּ לְרֵעֲךָ כָּמוֹךָ".

You should behave lovingly toward your fellow. That which you do not desire to be done to you, you should not do to your fellow. This is the meaning of "Love your fellow as yourself."

RABBI YEHUDAH BEN ELIEZER (RIVA)
CA. 13TH–14TH CENTURIES

Rabbi Yehudah lived in Troyes, France. In 1313, he authored *Minchat Yehudah*, a commentary on the Torah. This work often quotes Rabbi Ya'akov Tam, Rabbi Moshe of Courcy, and Chizkuni.

FULFILLING THE MITZVAH
SEEING YOURSELF
FROM GOD'S PERSPECTIVE

Text 5
MATTHEW MCKAY, PHD, AND PATRICK FANNING, *SELF-ESTEEM*
[OAKLAND, CA: NEW HARBINGER PUBLICATIONS, 2000], P. 2

Self-esteem is essential for psychological survival, it is an emotional *sine qua non*. . . .

Judging and rejecting yourself causes enormous pain. And in the same way that you would favor and protect a physical wound, you find yourself avoiding anything that might aggravate the pain of self-rejection in any way. You take fewer social, academic, or career risks. You make it more difficult for yourself to meet people, interview for a job, or push hard for something where you might not succeed. You limit your ability to open yourself with others . . . be the center of attention, hear criticism, ask for help, or solve problems.

To avoid more judgments and self-rejection, you erect barriers of defense. Perhaps you blame and get angry, or bury yourself in perfectionistic work. Or you brag. Or you make excuses. Sometimes you turn to alcohol or drugs.

MATTHEW MCKAY, PHD

Professor at the Wright Institute in Berkeley, CA. Mckay has authored and coauthored numerous books, including *The Relaxation and Stress Reduction Workbook, Self-Esteem, Thoughts and Feelings, When Anger Hurts,* and *Act on Life, Not on Anger.* McKay received his PhD in clinical psychology from the California School of Professional Psychology.

Question for Discussion

In what way(s) does low self-esteem hold you back in your life/relationships?

Exercise 1

A) Who are you? Describe yourself:

B) Who are you? Describe yourself (again).

Text 6

MISHNAH, SANHEDRIN 10:1

כָּל יִשְׂרָאֵל יֵשׁ לָהֶם חֵלֶק לְעוֹלָם הַבָּא, שֶׁנֶּאֱמַר: "וְעַמֵּךְ כּוּלָּם צַדִּיקִים לְעוֹלָם יִירְשׁוּ אָרֶץ, נֵצֶר מַטָּעַי מַעֲשֵׂה יָדַי לְהִתְפָּאֵר."

All of Israel have a share in the World to Come, as it is stated [Isaiah 60:21]: "And your people are all *tsadikim* [righteous]. They shall inherit the land forever. They are the branch of My planting, the work of My hands, in which I take pride."

MISHNAH

The first authoritative work of Jewish law that was codified in writing. The Mishnah contains the oral traditions that were passed down from teacher to student; it supplements, clarifies, and systematizes the commandments of the Torah. Due to the continual persecution of the Jewish people, it became increasingly difficult to guarantee that these traditions would not be forgotten. Rabbi Yehudah Hanasi therefore redacted the Mishnah at the end of the 2nd century. It serves as the foundation for the Talmud.

Text 7

RABBI TSADOK HAKOHEN RABINOWITZ, *TSIDKAT HATSADIK* 154

כְּשֵׁם שֶׁצָּרִיךְ אָדָם לְהַאֲמִין בְּהַשֵּׁם יִתְבָּרַךְ, כַּךְ צָרִיךְ אַחַר כַּךְ לְהַאֲמִין בְּעַצְמוֹ. רָצָה לוֹמַר, שֶׁיֵּשׁ לְהַשֵּׁם יִתְבָּרַךְ עֵסֶק עִמּוֹ וְשֶׁאֵינֶנּוּ פּוֹעֵל בָּטֵל . . . רַק צָרִיךְ לְהַאֲמִין כִּי נַפְשׁוֹ מִמְּקוֹר הַחַיִּים יִתְבָּרַךְ שְׁמוֹ, וְהַשֵּׁם יִתְבָּרֵךְ מִתְעַנֵּג וּמִשְׁתַּעֲשֵׁעַ בָּהּ כְּשֶׁעוֹשָׂה רְצוֹנוֹ.

Just as we must believe in God, we must also believe in ourselves. We must believe that God cares about us, that we are not worthless laborers . . . that we possess divine souls, and that God takes pleasure and joy when we fulfill His desire.

RABBI NACHUM ELIEZER RABINOWITZ

1928–

Israeli rabbi and Maimonidean scholar. Born in Montreal, Canada, Rabbi Rabinowitz received rabbinic ordination at Ner Israel, Baltimore, and a PhD in Philosophy of Science at the University of Toronto. An authority on Maimonides, he has published scientific, theological, and halachic works examining Maimonides' writings. He heads Yeshivat Birkat Moshe in Ma'ale Adumim, Israel.

SEEING OTHERS
FROM GOD'S PERSPECTIVE

Text 8

RABBI SHNE'UR ZALMAN OF LIADI, *TANYA*, CH. 32

וְלָכֵן נִקְרְאוּ כָּל יִשְׂרָאֵל אַחִים מַמָּשׁ, מִצַּד שֹׁרֶשׁ נַפְשָׁם בַּה'
אֶחָד, רַק שֶׁהַגּוּפִים מְחֻלָּקִים. וְלָכֵן הָעוֹשִׂים גּוּפָם עִקָּר וְנַפְשָׁם
טְפֵלָה, אִי אֶפְשָׁר לִהְיוֹת אַהֲבָה וְאַחֲוָה אֲמִתִּית בֵּינֵיהֶם, אֶלָּא
הַתְּלוּיָה בְּדָבָר לְבַדָּהּ.

ולכן העושים גופם עיקר ונפשם טפלה, אי אפשר להיות
אהבה ואחוה אמיתית ביניהם, אלא התלויה בדבר לבדה.

All Jews are considered actual brothers by virtue of the common source of their souls in the One God. It is only the bodies that are separate.

Therefore, those who give primary consideration to their bodily identity, while regarding their souls as of secondary importance, cannot experience true love and fraternity, only love that is predicated on personal benefit.

RABBI SHNE'UR ZALMAN OF LIADI (ALTER REBBE)
1745–1812

Chasidic rebbe, halachic authority, and founder of the Chabad movement. The Alter Rebbe was born in Liozna, Belarus, and was among the principal students of the Magid of Mezeritch. His numerous works include the *Tanya*, an early classic containing the fundamentals of Chabad Chasidism, and *Shulchan Aruch HaRav*, an expanded and reworked code of Jewish law.

Text 9

RABBI TZVI FREEMAN, *BRINGING HEAVEN DOWN TO EARTH II* (VANCOUVER, B.C.: CLASS ONE PRESS, 2007), P. 195

If you love yourself for your achievements, your current assets, the way you do things and handle the world—and despise yourself for failure in the same—it follows that your relationship with another will also be transient and superficial.

To achieve deep and lasting love of another person, you need to first experience the depth within yourself—an inner core that doesn't change with time or events. If it is the true essence, it is an essence shared by the other person as well, and deep love becomes unavoidable.

RABBI TZVI FREEMAN

1955–

Rabbi, computer scientist, and writer. A published expert, consultant, and lecturer in the field of educational technology, Rabbi Freeman held posts at the University of British Columbia and the Digipen School of Computer Gaming. Rabbi Freeman is the author of *Bringing Heaven Down to Earth* and *Men, Women & Kabbalah*. He is a senior editor at Chabad.org.

Exercise 2

In your own words, answer the following questions based on what we've learned.

1. *Love*: How can there be a command to "love"?

2. *Your fellow*: How can a person be expected to love every Jew, even a person they may not like, or don't even know?

3. *As yourself*: Is it possible to love anyone to such a degree?

UNDERSTANDING RABBI AKIVA AND HILLEL
SOUL-CONSCIOUSNESS VS. BODY-CONSCIOUSNESS

Text 10

RABBI SHNE'UR ZALMAN OF LIADI, *TANYA*, CH. 32

כִּי יְסוֹד וְשֹׁרֶשׁ כָּל הַתּוֹרָה הוּא לְהַגְבִּיהַּ וּלְהַעֲלוֹת הַנֶּפֶשׁ עַל הַגּוּף מַעְלָה.

For the foundation and root of the entire Torah is to prioritize and raise the soul high above the body.

LOVE OF GOD = LOVE OF ONE'S FELLOW

Text 11a
RABBI CHAIM VITAL, *SHA'AR HAKAVANOT, BIRKOT HASHACHAR*

קֹדֶם שֶׁהָאָדָם יְסַדֵּר תְּפִלָּתוֹ צָרִיךְ שֶׁיְּקַבֵּל עָלָיו מִצְוַת וְאָהַבְתָּ
לְרֵעֲךָ כָּמוֹךָ, וִיכַוֵּן לֶאֱהֹב כָּל אֶחָד מִבְּנֵי יִשְׂרָאֵל כְּנַפְשׁוֹ כִּי
עַל יְדֵי זֶה תַּעֲלֶה תְּפִלָּתוֹ כְּלוּלָה מִכָּל תְּפִלּוֹת יִשְׂרָאֵל וְתוּכַל
לַעֲלוֹת לְמַעֲלָה וְלַעֲשׂוֹת פְּרִי.

Before beginning to pray . . . one should accept the mitzvah to "love your fellow as yourself," and commit to love every Jew as he does his own soul. Through this, his prayer will be bound with the prayers of all other Jews, and it will be able to rise up and bear fruit.

RABBI CHAIM VITAL
CA. 1542–1620

Lurianic Kabbalist. Rabbi Vital was born in Israel, lived in Safed and Jerusalem, and later in Damascus. He was authorized by his teacher, Rabbi Yitschak Luria, the Arizal, to record his teachings. Acting on this mandate, Vital began arranging his master's teachings in written form, and his many works constitute the foundation of the Lurianic school of Jewish mysticism. His most famous work is *Ets Chaim*.

Text 11b
TEXT THAT APPEARS IN MANY *SIDDURIM*

הֲרֵינִי מְקַבֵּל עָלַי מִצְוַת עֲשֵׂה שֶׁל "וְאָהַבְתָּ לְרֵעֲךָ כָּמוֹךָ".

I hereby accept upon myself the mitzvah of "Love your fellow as yourself."

Question for Discussion

Why would affirming our relationship with others be considered a prerequisite to our relationship with God?

Text 12

RABBI YISRAEL BA'AL SHEM TOV CITED IN *HAYOM YOM* 5 IYAR

עֶס קומט אַרָאפּ אַ נְשָׁמָה אױף דֶער װעֶלט און לֶעבְט אָפּ זִיבעֶצִיג אַכְצִיג יָאהר, צוּלִיב טאָן אַ אִידעֶן אַ טוֹבָה בְּגַשְׁמיוּת וּבִפְרָט אִין רוּחְנִיוּת.

A soul may descend to this world and live seventy or eighty years just to do a Jew a material favor, and certainly a spiritual one.

RABBI YISRAEL BA'AL SHEM TOV (BESHT)

1698–1760

Founder of the Chasidic movement. Born in Slutsk, Belarus, the Ba'al Shem Tov was orphaned as a child. He served as a teacher's assistant and clay digger before founding the Chasidic movement and revolutionizing the Jewish world with his emphasis on prayer, joy, and love for every Jew, regardless of his or her level of Torah knowledge.

Figure 6.2

Practical Ways to Love Your Fellow Jew:

1. Start each morning by saying, "I accept upon myself the mitzvah to love my fellow Jew like myself."

2. Follow Hillel's golden rule: "If you wouldn't like it done to you, don't do it to the other guy."

3. Speak only good things about fellow Jews. Don't even listen to a bad word, unless some real benefit, or the avoidance of serious loss, will come through your conversation.

4. Care for your fellow Jew's property and possessions as you care for your own.

5. Always be on the lookout for opportunities to do another Jew a favor.

6. Bring Jewish people together. Tear down the false barriers of age, affiliation, and ethnicity.

7. Invite other Jews to share in the most precious thing we have, our Torah and *mitzvot*.

SHOULDN'T WE LOVE EVERYONE?

Question for Discussion

What makes the Jewish people, the Jewish people?

Text 13

RABBI TZVI FREEMAN, "BECAUSE WE ARE ALL ONE," CHABAD.ORG

Perhaps nothing has been as detrimental to the Jewish people as the modern idea that Judaism is a religion. If we are a religion, then some Jews are more Jewish, others less Jewish, and many Jews are not Jewish at all.

We are not a religion. We are a soul. A single soul radiating into many bodies, each ray shining forth on its unique mission, each body receiving the light according to its capacity, each embodiment playing its crucial role. Together we compose a symphony with no redundant parts, no instrument more vital than another. And our path back towards that original source of light is through every other ray that extends from it.

My Personal Take

In the space provided below, write down, in your own words, the two simple truths you learned in today's lesson.

"וְאָהַבְתָּ לְרֵעֲךָ "Love your fellow as yourself"
כָּמוֹךְ" – רַבִּי עֲקִיבָא (Leviticus 19:18). Rabbi
אוֹמֵר, "זֶה כְּלָל Akiva says this is a great
גָּדוֹל בַּתּוֹרה". principle of the Torah.

כָּל יִשְׂרָאֵל יֵשׁ All of Israel has a share in the
לָהֶם חֵלֶק לְעוֹלָם World to Come, as it is stated
הַבָּא, שֶׁנֶּאֱמַר: (Isaiah 60:21): "Your people are
"וְעַמֵּךְ כֻּלָּם צַדִּיקִים all righteous; they shall forever
לְעוֹלָם יִירְשׁוּ אָרֶץ, inherit the land. They are the
נֵצֶר מַטָּעַי מַעֲשֵׂה branch of My planting, the work of
יָדַי לְהִתְפָּאֵר". My hands, in which I take pride."

Key Points

1. When we peel away all the external layers that outwardly define us, there is so much more that unites us than that separates us.

2. The mitzvah to love one's fellow as oneself is a fundamental mitzvah of the Torah. However, this statement is perplexing for three reasons:

    (1) Love: How can there be a command to have an emotion?

    (2) Your fellow: How can a person to be expected to love every Jew, even those they may not even like, or don't even know?

    (3) As yourself: Is it possible to love anyone to such a degree?

3. We all possess a Godly core that constitutes our true identity as an incorruptible piece of God. It automatically follows that we are worthy of God's love and pride, no matter how we may act on the outside. This is our ultimate source of self-worth and self-love.

4. When we tap into and identify with this deepest part of our being, we are also tapping into the very essence of another's being, and thus we can love them as we love ourselves.

5. The goal of all of Torah is to "raise the soul high above the body"—to get in touch and identify with our souls, our Godly core. This perspective on life is manifest and epitomized in the extent to which we truly love and care for our fellow Jews.

6. The litmus test to determine the strength of one's relationship with God is the degree to which one loves others—and expresses that love in a practical sense.

Ephraim Wuensch, 2016

The Ultimate Mitzvah: Loving Your Fellow Jew

By Rabbi Manis Friedman

There are 613 mitzvos in the Torah. One is to feel the hunger of the poor, and therefore to give charity. Another is to feel the discomfort of a stranger, and therefore to show him hospitality. Not to be cruel, even to an animal, is another mitzvah. These commandments, though differing in their details are basically all expressions of concern, compassion and love. But the commandment of "Ahavas Yisroel"—to love your fellow Jew—seems to imply something beyond the above mentioned mitzvos. Because all of those are commandments relating to a specific act. What does the commandment to love a fellow Jew add to the commandments to be kind, generous, and compassionate? It adds the emphasis of loving EVERY Jew, and that the love itself is a mitzvah.

The Alter Rebbe, the first Lubavitcher Rebbe, said that to love another person means to find something in the other person that is similar to something in oneself. There are those parts of our lives and our existence that give us our individuality. These are the things that make each person different from another. And there are times when we must focus on our particular responsibility, our particular message in life. But the mitzvah of loving your fellow means being able to focus on those things that, rather than separating us, actually make us one. Once we discover that one thing which is universal to us all, we are in a position to love our fellow. "A Jew who sins and violates his Jewishness remains a Jew," says the Torah. A Jew is not created out of virtue. One doesn't become a Jew by doing mitzvos or good deeds. Faults, sins and misconduct do not stop one from being a Jew. A Jew remains a Jew no matter what. And, on the other hand, no matter how much good a Jew does, he remains a Jew (and not an angel). We see then that the state of being Jewish precedes any choices we are going to make. Long before we decide to put on *tefillin*, keep kosher, keep Shabbos or go to the *mikvah*, we are already Jewish. No matter what decisions we come to later in life, our Jewishness doesn't change, and it is not diminished.

What all Jews have in common is the part of G-d that He breathes into each person, the *neshama* (soul). Appreciating one's *neshama* allows a person to open himself up to every *neshama* in the world; this appreciation is a giant step toward loving every Jew. Because G-d has placed a part of Himself in every Jew, we are capable of loving every Jew. That which makes one person Jewish is exactly the same as that which makes every other Jew Jewish. If one loves that part of himself, then for the same reason he can love every other Jew. That is enough to make one person's heart miss a beat because of something that is happening to another.

The Alter Rebbe wrote that one's view of another person depends on how we see ourselves. If what is emphasized makes one different— namely, the human, physical condition—then one is incapable of loving. Not only can't he love every Jew, he can't love anybody. Because the most important thing to him is what makes him different, that which separates him from everybody. Focusing on differences separates people. The only way to be capable of loving is by making unimportant those things that make one different and separate. What must be primary is that which is shared with everybody else—the *neshama*, the soul.

In a similar vein:

Chassidus teaches that when a person has a problem in his spiritual growth and development, he should discuss it with someone else. He and the other person sit together and discuss a G-dly problem, so there are two G-dly souls against one animal soul (the animating force of the body)—the cause of the problem. At first glance this is difficult to comprehend. If you have two people, and therefore two G-dly souls, shouldn't you also have two animal souls? How can we possibly assert that the G-dly souls outnumber the animal?

However, when two G-dly souls get together they cooperate on a project. Two animal souls do not cooperate. It's against their nature to cooperate. An animal soul means a selfish soul. A selfish soul may want to sin, but it has no interest in helping anybody else sin. It gets no pleasure from anybody else's sins. Therefore, one animal soul will not join another animal soul in its sinfulness. But, a G-dly soul is naturally concerned and sympathetic to another G-dly soul. That is the nature of G-dly souls. So if one's animal being, human being, ego, is most important, then this person is separated from everybody else in the world. Nobody shares ego concerns, and if those are the things that are important to the person, then he's all alone. Or, as the Alter Rebbe said, he is incapable of loving -- unless it's for an ulterior motive. If, on the other hand, what is important is one's Jewishness, that feeling opens the person up to every other Jew. When the soul, which we all have in common, is emphasized, then we become one people, and it's literally possible to love every Jew.

How do we go about loving every Jew? In practical terms it means seeing through the differences that seem to separate one Jew from another. One can see beyond differences in culture and language. When two Jews meet in an airport, some place in the middle of Europe, and one doesn't speak Hebrew while the other doesn't speak English, still there's a feeling of kinship even though there's no way to communicate. One thing which often does confuse us, and sets up a barrier between Jews, is degrees of observance. The person who considers himself perfectly righteous and holy might feel that he has nothing in common with one whom he considers to be a sinful person. The sinful person, or the unlearned person, might feel that he has nothing in common with the scholarly saint. This difference between Jews is one that the Baal Shem Tov came to dispel in his teachings. The Baal Shem Tov taught two things. First, love your fellow Jew even if you've never seen him. You don't have to share any experiences, you don't have to share anything at all beyond the fact that you're Jewish. That in itself should be enough to create a bridge and a bond between one Jew and another.

The second teaching is that you have to love the wicked along with the righteous. Since we love a Jew because he's Jewish, not because he's righteous, then we love the Jew who is wicked, as well. The Baal Shem Tov said that "Love your fellow Jew as you love yourself," means to love the righteous and the wicked. The Alter Rebbe explained this concept further by saying that when the Baal Shem Tov said "the righteous and the wicked," he didn't mean that you certainly love the righteous, but you should also love the wicked along with the righteous. What he meant was that you love a Jew, period. You love your fellow Jew, and that's all that needs to be said. In practical terms, it means that you must relate to every Jew regardless of his behavior, personality, standing in society. But is that love? There is a connection that a fellow Jew feels for another Jew regardless of how the other person behaves. And no matter how strongly you disagree with the other's behavior, you cannot dismiss that other person, because he's your fellow Jew. To illustrate the point, you find that people who dress in the orthodox style, who happen to venture outside of their community, make other people very uncomfortable. But many people dress in very strange ways. You see Arabs of different religious orders in Israel who dress outlandishly. And yet, they walk up and down the streets of Jerusalem, and nobody pays any attention. But, should a Jew dressed in Chassidic garb, with a fur hat and long silk coat walk into a non-religious section, he gets angry stares. Why? Because he's dressed funny! Why is his dress any more funny or strange than the dress of the Arab *mullah*? It's not. It's just that the Arab is a stranger, and therefore he can dress however he wants.

When a Jew dresses strangely then every Jew cares. Even though a fellow Jew doesn't eat the same food or even act and believe the same, yet, if he dresses differently it makes us uncomfortable. Because he's a fellow Jew and Jews are not strangers to each other. The true bedrock of loving a fellow Jew is that one Jew cannot disassociate himself from another, no matter how much he would like to.

A story in the Gemara about the great sage Hillel will help clarify the above point. A man came to

Hillel and said that he wanted to be taught the whole Torah while standing on one foot. Hillel summed it all up for him by saying, "What is hateful to you, do not do to others. That is the whole Torah, the rest is commentary."

Hillel's statement doesn't appear anywhere in the Torah or Scriptures. The commentaries say that basically Hillel was referring to the mitzvah of "loving your fellow Jew as much as you love yourself." But, if that's the mitzvah he was referring to, why didn't he just say it? Why did Hillel make up this original statement?

If a person is impatient, and needs to be told something quickly, then what is said should be something definitive. Hillel gave the man a very vague answer, which needed a great deal of thought before being put into practice.

The Tzemach Tzedek, the third Lubavitcher Rebbe, explained that what Hillel was really saying was very clearly defined and practical. A person can admit his own faults, and see them very clearly, and even talk about them publicly. Yet, if another person would point out those weaknesses, the first person would be insulted and very hurt. Why can one honestly admit to a fault within himself, yet that same person becomes offended when it is pointed out to him? The difference is that when one sees his own faults it is within a certain context. Having assured himself of being a worthwhile creature, a person can proceed to search out his faults. Even talking about them to others doesn't do any damage. But when somebody else sees the faults, it's not necessarily within that framework of already knowing that the person is a worthwhile human being. We are concerned that any personality flaw suggests total insignificance. We fear criticism only because we're afraid it might lead to rejection. Were it not for that, we would be very comfortable hearing and accepting criticism. We can't honestly deny every criticism we hear; they're all true to some degree. It doesn't do any damage to the ego to admit that we're not the smartest or the prettiest, or the strongest or most talented. That which hurts, that which is hateful, is to have our faults pointed out by someone who is not necessarily convinced that we are worthwhile human beings.

When Hillel said to this man, "What is hateful to you, don't do to others," he was being very specific. He was talking about that thing which is hateful. Not "whatever" is hateful, but *that* which is hateful to you do not do to others. "That thing" is seeing another person's fault, without first recognizing his worth. That's what we hate and what we shouldn't do to others. What Hillel was doing for this man was summing up all of the Torah in one mitzvah, the mitzvah of "loving a fellow Jew as much as you love yourself." Since the man was very impatient, and seemingly not very ambitious, if Hillel had told him, "love your fellow Jew as much as you love yourself," he would have thought it was impossible, too demanding. So Hillel translated it for him into practical terms. You can't measure the amount you love yourself. In self-love, before you see your own faults you already know that you are important, significant. No matter what your body and human personality turn out to be, your *neshama* is already valuable. And with that knowledge and security you can look at your faults and not be hurt. That's how you love yourself: you consider yourself worthwhile despite your faults; you must know that your fellow Jew is worthwhile, too. No matter how the other Jew behaves, there is something very valuable about this person—the very fact that he is a Jew.

The Lubavitcher Rebbe once said, that when talking to another Jew, you have to realize that every Jew is an only child to G-d, the King of Kings. Therefore, when you talk to another Jew, you have to keep in mind whose child this is, even if he doesn't behave like the child of the King of Kings, you have to remember who his Father is.

G-d created the world very carefully and thoughtfully. Everything we see and hear is of meaning to us. If G-d allows us to see the faults of another person, He is showing an opportunity to fulfill the purpose for which we were created. When we see another person's faults, our first reaction has to be, "What are we being told?" Seeing the other person's faults can mean that he will not improve his behavior unless we help him, because that's the way G-d set it up. Because, if G-d is letting you see this fault, it must be your job to help him fix it. The second possibility is that the fault is in you, and you're seeing it reflected in the other person. A fault in another person should elicit the reaction, "What's that got to do with me? Why do I need to see this?" The other person's fault offers us the opportunity to improve, to show us something in ourselves that we are not seeing. Therefore, we are indebted to the other person even if his fault consists of hurting us. This person is the messenger through whom this enlightenment is coming and there is no need to be hateful.

The ultimate part in love of a fellow Jew is that every Jew has a Divine soul, and regardless of how he behaves, that soul remains. Where do we see the evidence of this G-dly soul? Love of a fellow Jew, taken to its fullest expression, is the ability to discover evidence, signs of the presence of a Divine soul, even in a person who does not, at first glance, seem to have any soul at all. In pursuing the mitzvah of loving your fellow Jew, we start with the awareness that every Jew is a little piece of G-d, and that if that piece of G-d is not evident in the person's life, then it is your job to reveal it. To help that person discover his own G-dliness. Bringing ourselves together, being able to see past the externals and faults, to be aware of the *neshama* of a Jew, is what heals the wound of Exile, and brings *Moshiach*.

Blood Brothers

By Rabbi Elisha Greenbaum

Mel Brooks has a line in one of his "Two-Thousand-Year-Old Man" routines where he is asked to define "tragedy."

"Say I was to cut my finger, well, that's tragic, terrible. It hurts! But if you were to trip over and drop dead on the spot, big deal, what do I care? It's not my problem!"

Contrast that to *"Love your fellow as yourself; I am G-d."* (Leviticus 19:18). The verse demands one demonstrate love for another Jew equal to one's love of self. The blood trickling down your finger should be as tragically disturbing to me as when staunching my own wound, and the caring and consideration I demand for my own feelings I must demonstrate in my attitude to you.

How is it possible to truly *love another as oneself*? By remembering *I am G-d*, equating the act of love for one's brethren to love of one's G-d. The intrinsic soul connection of a Jew to his G-d (demonstrated by the absolute refusal of even the most assimilated among us to consider abandoning Judaism completely) is replicated in the soul connection between Jews. To reject another Jew, is the equivalent of renouncing G-d.

WHAT IS YOUR PRIORITY?

Draw a mental portrait of yourself (feel free to drop a few years and pounds). Now add to your picture a traditional Yemenite Jew replete with dark skin, curly *peyos* and long flowing caftan. Good, now go black and white: a *chassid* in uniform. Whack in an Ethiopian; a big bellied, bum-bag toting, loud-mouthed American tourist; a *kova tembel*-ed Israeli farmer dancing a *hora* around his orange trees and a few other members of the tribe, of various appearances and persuasions. Now let me ask you, what "tribe"?

What earthly resemblance do any of these comic book characters have to you or your lifestyle? You share no language, cultural background, pigmentation or interests with any of the above. Yet they are family. Were, G-d forbid, misfortune to befall them, the ties which bind us would elicit your immediate help and sympathy and, when needed, your voice would be raised in their defense just as quickly as would theirs in yours.

Think of your nuclear family. My affection for my siblings is absolute. We share bloodlines, parents and genes. Living on separate continents, with disparate interests and lifestyles, does not diminish that affinity, nor weaken those bonds.

Similarly between Jews; our differences are physical, our commonalities, spiritual. Superficially we may look dissimilar but our matching denominator is our common soul. The Jewish soul is an undifferentiated part of G-d, untarnished and resolute, held in trust within us, the life force of our earthly existence. From a soul perspective we are more than brothers, we are identical twins, with a common father, G-d. When one's emphasis is the soul, one can truly achieve equality and harmony between all Jews. The identical spiritual DNA we carry is the code to our common destiny and the primary drive for the sense of love and kinship Jews bear for each other.

Better Is a World Built on Love, Not Darwinian Struggle

By Rabbi Jonathan Sacks, PhD

The word "credo," in Hebrew *ani ma'amin*, means "I believe," and it sometimes helps to spell out what we believe, why we do what we do, and why we are what we are. This, briefly, is my credo.

I believe that life has a meaning, that neither we nor the universe are here by sheer happenstance. The search for meaning is definitive of the human condition, for we are the only life forms yet known in all the vast universe capable of asking the question "why?"

From this, something momentous follows. The meaning of any system lies outside the system. The meaning of chess—why people play it, and why some devote their lives to it—is not to be found in the rules of chess. They tell us how the game works, not why it is played. The meaning of a credit card is not to be found in its physical properties, the plastic of which it is made and the markings it carries. The internal workings of any system do not explain the place the system holds in human lives.

If, then, the meaning of a system lies outside the system, then the meaning of the universe lies outside the universe. That is the revolution of Abrahamic monotheism. Monotheism is not about the mere mathematical reduction of many gods to One. It is the leap of transcendence that for the first time conceives of a reality beyond the universe. This alone has the power to redeem life from tragedy and meaninglessness.

Since we are creatures of the universe, that meaning will always be imperfectly understood. At best we have intimations. Yet history has given us those rare souls whose inner ear was attuned to a deeper music: the prophets and patriarchs, sages and saints who heard the call of the beyond—within that is the voice of God in the human heart.

If the universe was brought into being by One beyond the universe, then it was created by a being who desires to bring things into being. The simplest way of expressing this is: God created the universe in love. For it is love that seeks to bring new life into being. It is love that makes space for the other. God's love made space for the universe and for that astonishing sequence of events that produced us.

If so, then each of us is here because of God's love. That fact transforms the human condition, rescuing it from ultimate solitude. We are not alone. We exist because someone wanted us to be, someone who believes in us even when we lose belief in ourselves, who knows our fears and hears our prayers, giving us strength when we falter and lifting us when we fall.

And just as God creates in love so he asks us to create in love. The Abrahamic monotheisms are the only systems to place love at the heart of the moral life. There are other codes of ethics: every civilization has them, whether they are secular or religious. All civilizations have something like the golden rule: treat others as you would wish to be treated. Many of them have forms of justice: treat equals equally. But only a vision that sees the world as God's work of love, makes love the highest value. Love God with all your heart, soul and might. Love your neighbour as yourself. Love the stranger for you know what it feels like to be a stranger.

And yes, there is another way of seeing the world and our place within it. The universe came into being for no reason, and one day for no reason it will cease to be. There is nothing special about humanity: we are mere primates with a gift for language. There is nothing special about any of us. We are born, we live, we die, and it is as if we had never been. Our ideals are illusions; our hopes mere dreams.

We have no souls, only brains; no freedom, only the hardwiring of our genes. And the biggest illusion of them all is love, the smokescreen created by humans to hide the fact that we are here to reproduce.

I know which I prefer. Better is a world built on love than on the Darwinian struggle to survive. Greater the mind that lifts its eyes beyond the visible horizon than one that refuses to believe anything that cannot be measured, mapped and scientifically explained.

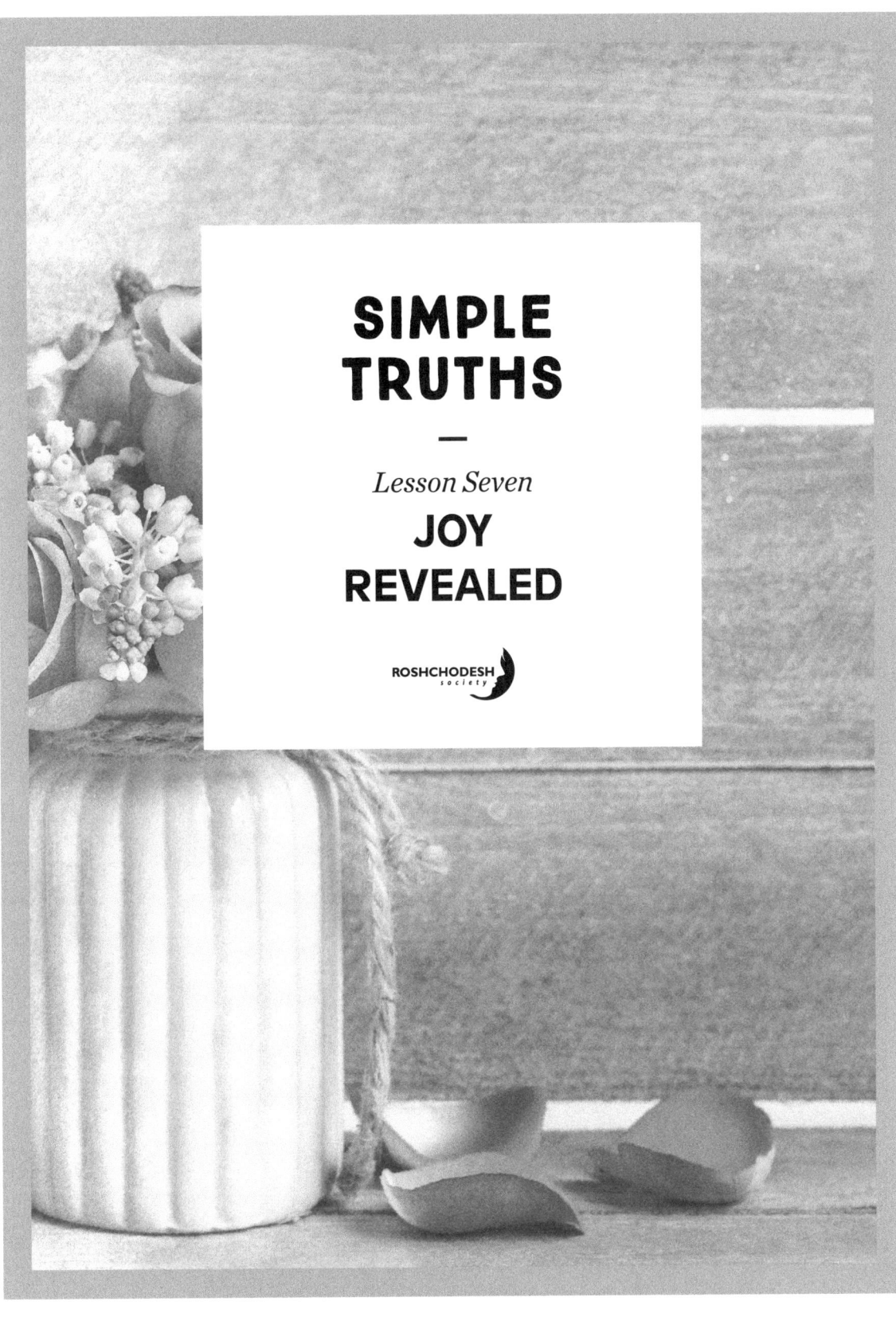

SIMPLE TRUTHS

—

Lesson Seven

JOY REVEALED

ROSHCHODESH
society

| 168

THE HAPPINESS ADVANTAGE

Questions for Discussion

1.   What brings you joy?

2.   Why do these things bring you joy?

Text 1

RABBI SHOLOM DOVBER OF LUBAVITCH, *SEFER HAMA'AMARIM* 5657, P. 224

שִׂמְחָה פּוֹרֵץ גֶּדֶר.

Joy breaks through boundaries.

RABBI SHALOM DOVBER SCHNEERSOHN (RASHAB)
1860–1920

Chasidic rebbe. Rabbi Shalom Dovber became the fifth leader of the Chabad movement upon the passing of his father, Rabbi Shmuel of Lubavitch. He established the Lubavitch network of *yeshivot* called Tomchei Temimim. He authored many volumes of chasidic discourses and is renowned for his lucid and thorough explanations of kabbalistic concepts.

Question for Discussion

What do you think is meant by this statement?

ROSH CHODESH SOCIETY / SIMPLE TRUTHS

Text 2

SUNIYA S. LUTHAR, PHD, "THE CULTURE OF AFFLUENCE: PSYCHOLOGICAL COSTS OF MATERIAL WEALTH," *CHILD DEVELOPMENT* 74:6 (2003)

One of the first empirical studies to provide a glimpse into problems of affluent youth was a comparative investigation of low-income, urban 10th graders and their upper socioeconomic status (SES), suburban counterparts. . . . The sample included 264 suburban students who were mostly from Caucasian, white-collar families, and 224 inner-city youth who were predominantly minority and of low SES. . . . Affluent youth reported significantly higher levels of anxiety across several domains, and greater depression. They also reported significantly higher substance use than inner-city students, consistently indicating more frequent use of cigarettes, alcohol, marijuana, and other illicit drugs.

SUNIYA SUNANDA LUTHAR PHD

Professor of psychology. Luthar is currently at Arizona State University and is professor emerita at Columbia University's Teachers College. Her books include *Children in Poverty, Developmental Psychopathology,* and *Resilience and Vulnerability in Childhood.* She served as associate editor of the journal *Developmental Psychology,* and currently serves as associate editor for the journal *Development and Psychopathology.*

Text 3

TIKUNEI ZOHAR 22

וְאַתְוָון בְּשִׂמְחָ"ה אִיהִי מַחֲשָׁבָ"ה.

TIKUNEI ZOHAR

An appendix to the Zohar, the seminal work of Kabbalah (Jewish mysticism). *Tikunei Zohar* consists mostly of seventy Kabbalistic expositions on the opening verse of the Torah. It was first printed in Mantua in 1558.

The letters forming the Hebrew word *"besimchah"* (with joy) are the same letters that spell *"machshavah"* (thought).

A LIGHT TO THE NATIONS

Text 4

ISAIAH 60:3

וְהָלְכוּ גוֹיִם לְאוֹרֵךְ, וּמְלָכִים לְנֹגַהּ זַרְחֵךְ.

Nations shall go by your [Israel's] light and kings by the glow of your radiance.

Questions for Discussion

1. What is the nature of the "light" to which Isaiah refers; what is our message to the world?

2. By what methods do we transmit this illuminating message to the people of the world?

3. In your estimation, what has been Judaism's greatest contribution to society?

HABITAT CREATION
FIRST THINGS FIRST

Text 5

MIDRASH, *BEREISHIT RABAH* 44:1

לֹא נִתְּנוּ הַמִּצְוֹת אֶלָּא לְצָרֵף בָּהֶן אֶת הַבְּרִיּוֹת.

God gave us the *mitzvot* because they effect the refinement of humankind.

BEREISHIT RABAH

An early rabbinic commentary on the Book of Genesis. This Midrash bears the name of Rabbi Oshiya Rabah (Rabbi Oshiya "the Great") whose teaching opens this work. This Midrash provides textual exegeses and stories, expounds upon the biblical narrative, and develops and illustrates moral principles. Produced by the sages of the Talmud in the Land of Israel, its use of Aramaic closely resembles that of the Jerusalem Talmud. It was first printed in Constantinople in 1512 together with four other Midrashic works on the other four books of the Pentateuch.

Text 6

MIDRASH, *SHOCHAR TOV*, PSALMS 90:4

אַלְפַּיִם שָׁנָה קָדְמָה תוֹרָה לִבְרִיָּתוֹ שֶׁל עוֹלָם.

The Torah preceded the creation of the world by two thousand years.

SHOCHAR TOV (MIDRASH TEHILLIM)

is an Aggadic Midrash on Psalms, containing homilies on verses and individual words. It is an old work, known since the 11th century when it was cited by Rashi and other scholars.

HOUSE VS. HOME

Text 7

RABBI SHNE'UR ZALMAN OF LIADI, *TANYA*, CHAPTER 33

וְזֶה כָּל הָאָדָם, וְתַכְלִית בְּרִיאָתוֹ וּבְרִיאַת כָּל הָעוֹלָמוֹת, עֶלְיוֹנִים
וְתַחְתּוֹנִים, לִהְיוֹת לוֹ יִתְבָּרֵךְ דִּירָה זוֹ בְּתַחְתּוֹנִים.

The purpose of the creation of every human being and of all the worlds is for God to have a home
in this lowly realm..

RABBI SHNEUR ZALMAN OF LIADI (ALTER REBBE)

1745–1812

Chasidic rebbe, halachic authority, and founder of the Chabad movement. The Alter Rebbe was born in Liozna, Belarus, and was among the principal students of the Magid of Mezeritch. His numerous works include the *Tanya*, an early classic containing the fundamentals of Chabad Chasidism, and *Shulchan Aruch HaRav*, an expanded and reworked code of Jewish law.

Question for Discussion

What is the difference between a "house" and a "home"?

SYNCING THE WORLD

Text 8

PRESIDENT JOHN ADAMS, FROM A LETTER TO F. A. VAN DER
KEMP (1808), PENNSYLVANIA HISTORICAL SOCIETY

The Jewish people have civilized humanity more than any other nation in history. I will insist the Hebrews have done more to civilize men than any other nation. If I was an atheist and believed in blind eternal fate, I should still believe that fate had ordained the Jews to be the most essential instrument for civilizing the nations. . . . They are the most glorious nation that ever inhabited this earth. The Romans and their empire were but a bauble in comparison to the Jews. They have given religion to three-quarters of the globe and have influenced the affairs of mankind more, and more happily than any other nation, ancient or modern.

JOHN ADAMS
1735–1826

Second president of the United States and political theorist. Adams, a Boston lawyer and public figure, was an active and influential leader in the American Revolution and helped Thomas Jefferson draft the Declaration of Independence. Adams served two terms as George Washington's vice president before being elected president.

Text 9

ORECHOT TSADIKIM, SHA'AR HANEDIVUT

יֵשׁ שְׁלוֹשָׁה מִינֵי נְדִיבוּת. הָאֶחָד, נָדִיב בַּמָּמוֹן. הַשֵּׁנִי, נָדִיב
בַּגוּף. הַשְּׁלִישִׁי, נָדִיב בְּחָכְמָה. וְאֵלוּ הַשְּׁלוֹשָׁה הָיוּ בְּאַבְרָהָם
אָבִינוּ.

שֶׁהָיָה נָדִיב בַּמָּמוֹן, דִּכְתִיב (בְּרֵאשִׁית כא, לג), "וַיִּטַּע אֶשֶׁל".
נָדִיב בְּגוּפוֹ, שֶׁהִצִּיל לוֹט בֶּן אָחִיו וְנִלְחַם עֲבוּרוֹ. נָדִיב בְּחָכְמָתוֹ,
כִּי לִמֵּד לְכָל הָעָם הַדֶּרֶךְ הַיָּשָׁר עַד שֶׁנִתְגַּיְּירוּ, דִּכְתִיב (שָׁם יב,
ה), "וְאֶת הַנֶּפֶשׁ אֲשֶׁר עָשׂוּ בְחָרָן".

ORECHOT TSADIKIM

A classic work on Jewish ethics. The identity of the author is unknown, but it is believed to have been written by a French scholar, probably in the 14th century. Drawing much from earlier ethicists Solomon ibn Gabirol, Maimonides, and Bachya ibn Pakuda, *Orechot Tsadikim* ("The Ways of the Righteous") focuses on refining character traits and maintaining a balance in all matters.

There are three types of generosity: Generosity with one's money, generosity with one's time and effort, and generosity with one's wisdom. Our forefather Abraham possessed all of them.

His monetary generosity is indicated in the verse (Genesis 21:33), "Abraham planted a [hospitality] tent [in Beersheba]." He demonstrated his willingness to personally help others when he went to battle to rescue his nephew Lot. He was generous with his wisdom and taught the proper path to his countrymen, causing them to convert, as the verse says (Genesis 12:5), "[Abram took his wife Sarai . . .] and the souls that they had obtained in Haran, [and they made their way toward the land of Canaan]."

Text 10

MAIMONIDES, *MISHNEH TORAH*, LAWS OF KINGS 9:1

עַל שִׁשָּׁה דְּבָרִים נִצְטַוָּוה אָדָם הָרִאשׁוֹן: עַל עֲבוֹדָה זָרָה, וְעַל
בִּרְכַּת הַשֵּׁם, וְעַל שְׁפִיכוּת דָּמִים, וְעַל גִּלּוּי עֲרָיוֹת, וְעַל הַגֶּזֶל,
וְעַל הַדִּינִים. .. הוֹסִיף לְנֹחַ אֵבֶר מִן הַחַי.

God gave Adam six rules [that he and his descendants were to follow. God outlawed]: (1) idolatry, (2) blaspheme, (3) murder, (4) illicit sexual relationships, and (5) theft; and [He instructed him to] (6) establish a judiciary.... To Noah, God added [another prohibition]: (7) [consuming] a limb [that was torn off] of a live animal.

RABBI MOSHE BEN MAIMON (MAIMONIDES, RAMBAM)

1135–1204

Halachist, philosopher, author, and physician. Maimonides was born in Cordoba, Spain. After the conquest of Cordoba by the Almohads, he fled Spain and eventually settled in Cairo, Egypt. There, he became the leader of the Jewish community and served as court physician to the vizier of Egypt. He is most noted for authoring the *Mishneh Torah*, an encyclopedic arrangement of Jewish law, and for his philosophical work, *Guide for the Perplexed*. His rulings on Jewish law are integral to the formation of halachic consensus.

UN-APOCALYPSE

Text 11

MAIMONIDES, *MISHNEH TORAH*, LAWS OF KINGS 12:1–2

אַל יַעֲלֶה עַל הַלֵּב שֶׁבִּימוֹת הַמָּשִׁיחַ יְבֻטַּל דָּבָר מִמִּנְהָגוֹ שֶׁל עוֹלָם אוֹ יִהְיֶה שָׁם חִדּוּשׁ בְּמַעֲשֵׂה בְרֵאשִׁית, אֶלָּא עוֹלָם כְּמִנְהָגוֹ נוֹהֵג . . . אָמְרוּ חֲכָמִים, "אֵין בֵּין הָעוֹלָם הַזֶּה לִימוֹת הַמָּשִׁיחַ אֶלָּא שִׁעְבּוּד מַלְכֻיּוֹת בִּלְבַד".

Do not presume that the Messianic Era will feature changes in the way the world operates or any modifications to the laws of nature. Rather, the world will continue to operate as it always has. . . . Our sages taught: "The only difference between the current age and the Messianic era is that we will be then be freed from subjugation to foreign regimes."

Text 12

ISAIAH 2:4

וְכִתְּתוּ חַרְבוֹתָם לְאִתִּים, וַחֲנִיתוֹתֵיהֶם לְמַזְמֵרוֹת. לֹא יִשָּׂא גוֹי אֶל גּוֹי חֶרֶב, וְלֹא יִלְמְדוּ עוֹד מִלְחָמָה.

The nations will beat their swords into plowshares and their spears into pruning hooks;

Nation will not lift up sword against nation, and never more will they study warfare.

GOD'S PUBLICISTS

Text 13a
GENESIS 21:33

וַיִּטַּע אֶשֶׁל בִּבְאֵר שָׁבַע, וַיִּקְרָא שָׁם בְּשֵׁם ה' אֵ-ל עוֹלָם.

Abraham planted a tent in Beer-Sheba, and he proclaimed (Hebrew: *vayikra*) there in the name of God, Lord of the world.

Text 13b
TALMUD, SOTAH 10A–B

אַל תִּיקְרֵי "וַיִּקְרָא" אֶלָא "וַיַּקְרִיא", מְלַמֵּד שֶׁהִקְרִיא אַבְרָהָם אָבִינוּ לִשְׁמוֹ שֶׁל הַקָּדוֹשׁ בָּרוּךְ הוּא בְּפֶּה כָּל עוֹבֵר וְשָׁב.

Do not read *vayikra*—"he proclaimed"—but rather *vayakri*—"he caused others to proclaim." This teaches that Abraham our forefather caused the name of God to be proclaimed by every passerby.

THE JOY OF PURPOSE

Text 14
RABBI SHNE'UR ZALMAN OF LIADI, *TANYA*, CH. 33

יִשְׂמַח יִשְׂרָאֵל בְּעוֹשָׂיו, פֵּרוּשׁ שֶׁכָּל מִי שֶׁהוּא מִזֶּרַע יִשְׂרָאֵל יֵשׁ
לוֹ לִשְׂמֹחַ בְּשִׂמְחַת ה', אֲשֶׁר שָׂשׂ וְשָׂמֵחַ בְּדִירָתוֹ בְּתַחְתּוֹנִים.

"Israel should rejoice in its Maker" (Psalms 149:2). Every member of Israel ought to share in God's joy and happiness, which He derives from His dwelling place in this lowly realm.

My Personal Take

In the space provided below, write down, in your own words, the two simple truths you learned in today's lesson.

יִשְׂמַח יִשְׂרָאֵל בְּעוֹשָׂיו, "Israel should rejoice in its Maker" (Psalms 149:2). Every member of Israel ought to share in God's joy and happiness, which He derives from His dwelling place in this lowly realm.

פֵּרוּשׁ: שֶׁכָּל מִי שֶׁהוּא מִזֶּרַע יִשְׂרָאֵל יֵשׁ לוֹ לִשְׂמֹחַ בְּשִׂמְחַת ה', אֲשֶׁר שָׂשׂ וְשָׂמֵחַ בְּדִירָתוֹ בְּתַחְתּוֹנִים.

וְזֶה כָּל הָאָדָם וְתַכְלִית בְּרִיאָתוֹ וּבְרִיאַת כָּל הָעוֹלָמוֹת, עֶלְיוֹנִים וְתַחְתּוֹנִים, לִהְיוֹת לוֹ יִתְבָּרֵךְ דִּירָה זוֹ בְּתַחְתּוֹנִים.

The purpose of the creation of every human being and of all the worlds is for God to have a home in this lowly realm.

Key Points

1. Torah contains not only the tools to successfully navigate the issues we face in our current reality, but it provides us with the tools to bring ourselves and the world to a greater reality.

2. As Jews, we are not content with leading personally healthy and wholesome lives. We have a responsibility to the entire world: to serve as "a light to the nations."

3. Our task is to transform this lowly world into a "home for God." For this world to be God's home, it needs to become a place of goodness, morality, and holiness, a place that reflects God's values, wishes, and preferences. We accomplish this through utilizing every element of creation in our service of God.

4. For the world to be God's home, it needs to be in synch with divine values. Hence we are tasked with teaching the world the "Seven Noahide Laws"—the universal moral rules of God's "home."

5. Influencing the world to be in synch with divine values, as expressed in the Torah, is a prelude to the proliferation of the knowledge of God.

6. The Chasidic masters explain that joy releases us from our personal limitations and unleashes the full power of our talents and strengths. While to some degree our circumstances can impact our happiness, we all have the ability to orient our thinking in ways that will increase our feelings of joy.

7. Taking part in our national mission and destiny gives us the ultimate and most lasting form of joy—a joy that stems from a profound sense of privilege and accomplishment. This joy is also the fuel that energizes us to fulfill this mission.

8. The greatest source of joy is identifying with the joy that God Himself derives from our work in creating His terrestrial habitat. This level of joy bespeaks the deepest level of oneness with God that we can possibly experience.

APPENDICES

Appendix A

THOMAS CAHILL, *THE GIFT OF THE JEWS: HOW A TRIBE OF DESERT NOMADS CHANGED THE WAY EVERYONE THINKS AND FEELS* (NEW YORK: NAN A. TALESE, 1999.), P. 5

All evidence points to there having been, in the earliest religious thought, a vision of the cosmos that was profoundly cyclical. The assumptions that early man made about the world were, in all their essentials, little different from the assumptions that later and more sophisticated societies, like Greece and India, would make in a more elaborate manner. As Henri-Charles Puech says of Greek thought in his seminal *Man and Time*: "No event is unique, nothing is enacted but once . . .; every event has been enacted, is enacted, and will be enacted perpetually; the same individuals have appeared, appear, and will appear at every turn of the circle."

The Jews were the first people to break out of this circle, to find a new way of thinking and experiencing, a new way of understanding and feeling the world, so much so that it may be said with some justice that theirs is the only new idea that human beings have ever had. But their worldview has become so much a part of us that at this point it might as well have been written into our cells as a genetic code.

THOMAS CAHILL

1940– American scholar and writer. Born in New York City to Irish-American parents, Cahill has a pontifical degree in philosophy, and an MFA in film and dramatic literature from Columbia University. Cahill has taught at Queens College, Fordham University, and Seton Hall University. He is best known for *The Hinges of History* series, in which he recounts formative moments in Western civilization.

Appendix B

IBID., PP. 240–241

We can hardly get up in the morning or cross the street without being Jewish. We dream Jewish dreams and hope Jewish hopes. Most of our best words, in fact—*new, adventure, surprise; unique, individual, person, vocation; time, history, future; freedom, progress, spirit; faith, hope, justice*—are the gifts of the Jews.

What Does G-d Need Us For?

By Rabbi Aron Moss

Rabbi, I have two questions for you:
1) Do you make up these questions or do you receive them from real people?
2) If G-d is perfect, why did He create us? A perfect being isn't missing anything, so why would He need us? And if He doesn't need us, is our life meaningless? Are we just some divine experiment?

ANSWER:

Some questions are too esoteric to answer. It is beyond our limited understanding to reach a solution to all the mysteries of the universe, and these may always remain mysteries. So I will have to skip your first question and only deal with the second.

You are absolutely correct: G-d, being perfect, was missing nothing before creation. There is no possible need that this world can fulfill for Him. He doesn't need anything.

So creating us could not have been in order to fulfill a need. It was something G-d chose to do. He doesn't need us, He wants us.

What does G-d want from us? The one thing He didn't have before creation was a relationship. He was alone. What He wanted from this world was a relationship with free beings. So He created us and gave us ways of connecting to Him—the mitzvot.

But we can't say that He *needed* this relationship with us. He may have been alone before creation, but he was still G-d—perfect and missing nothing. He didn't need a relationship—He wanted it.

Does this make our life unnecessary? Does the fact that G-d doesn't "need" us make us less significant?

No, on the contrary. When we have a relationship with someone just because we need them (such as a cleaning lady, or a family doctor) then when that need has been fulfilled the relationship ends. Your connection is dependent on them providing a service, and will only last as long as that service is needed.

But when we have a relationship with someone simply because we want to, because we have chosen to connect to them, then that bond is intrinsic. We don't love them because of what they do for us, we love them for who they are—and that is forever.

G-d doesn't need us; He wants us. He didn't give us commandments because He needs them to be fulfilled, but because He wants us to relate to Him. If we were created because G-d needed us to do something, then we would be secondary to that mission—once the mission was fulfilled we could be disposed of. But G-d needs nothing. He chose to bring us into being as a pure act of love. That is the test of true love: if my beloved could no longer provide me with my needs, would I still love him or her just for being my beloved? By creating us, G-d answered yes.

Happiness Is Being There:
About the One Act in Life That Is Perfectly Still

By Rabbi Tzvi Freeman

Fools we were. In the womb, all was warm, all was provided. In the womb, we could just *be*. What were we missing that we had to squeeze our way through the birth canal, to break out into this cold world? Because from that point on, there is no rest, only movement, constant movement.

That is what life beyond the womb is all about: getting somewhere. And as soon as you are there, getting somewhere else. Scurrying down one corridor to arrive at a doorway to yet another corridor where we must furiously seek out the next doorway. When are we ever in a place for the sake of being in that place? What do we ever do for the sake of doing? Even in the moment of pleasure we yearn for a greater pleasure, until "no one leaves this world with half his desire in his hand."[1] When can we ever once again just *be*?

If so for the materialist, how much more so for the seeker of knowledge, of wisdom, of spiritual growth. "The students of the sages have no rest," the Talmud informs us. "They are continually moving from strength to strength."[2] The Zohar describes Abraham, constantly traveling "southward"—meaning, towards the light. And as close as you come, the light, an infinite light, becomes yet more distant, more unattainable.[3]

Yet a mitzvah is just that: being *There*, having *The Thing Itself*—not the light, but the *Source of Light*. Not because you have come closer to that Source, not because you are holding it in your hands, but because that Source and you have become one.[4]

Why is this? Because the Essence of All Things speaks gently to you and asks, "Please be My hands, My feet, My mind. Be My presence within your material world. All that I have made, I have made as a stage upon which My innermost desire may unfold, and that most precious drama I have left for you."

You follow the choreography for which you were formed within your mother's womb, this mitzvah that has come your way, in its particular way in your particular world. And in that act, the two of you have become one—you, the tiny creature, and He, the Infinite Creator. The same innermost desire breathes within each of you.[5]

Why can't you feel it? Because the physical body and the material world—and even the soul as it is compressed into that body—cannot sustain such a degree of ecstasy. When the people received the Torah at Mt. Sinai, with each statement, their souls took flight from their bodies. Even to feel just a glimmer of that energy, the soul must ascend back to its heavenly origin and yet higher—and there it will need the special protection afforded it by its mitzvot so as not to dissipate within the all-encompassing light.

"I was a boor and I had no knowledge," sings the psalmist about our predicament carrying out our mission in this world. "I was like a beast with You. Yet I was constantly with You . . ."[6] In a time to come, we will have bodies capable of sustaining the ecstasy of conscious union

1. Kohelet Rabbah 1:34.
2. Talmud, Berachot 64a and Moed Katan 29a.
3. See Zohar, Lech Lecha 80a; Tanya, Likkutei Amarim, chapter 47; Torah Ohr 66d.
4. Likkutei Torah, Devarim 1b. See also Derech Mitzvotecha, Mitzvat Pru Urvu.
5. See Tanya, Likkutei Amarim, chs. 4 and 23.
6. Psalms 73:22. See Tanya, Likkutei Amarim, end of chapter 46.

with The Thing Itself. In the meantime, the closest we can come to that ecstasy is the celebration of each mitzvah as we act it through. In that joy of a mitzvah, taught the Baal Shem Tov, is an infinite reward beyond anything the highest spiritual world can contain.[7] In that joy, you have returned to the very womb of all being.

---

7.   Keter Shem Tov 129; from Toldot Yaakov Yosef, Kedoshim, p. 336b.

ACKNOWLEDGMENTS

Seldom does one have the opportunity to seamlessly fuse a life's mission and a labor of love. These acknowledgments are a public affirmation of the incredible blessings I experience daily.

Extreme appreciation is owed to the course editor, **Mrs. Chava Shapiro,** for her exemplary dedication, talent, and excellent skills in bringing this project to fruition. I am deeply grateful to our gifted writers, **Mrs. Zeldy Friedman, Mrs. Chava Shapiro**, and **Rabbi Michoel Shapiro** for authoring this course with wisdom, wit, and brilliant insight. Much gratitude goes to **Rabbi Mendel Rubin** for the unique creativity he contributed to this curriculum.

We are grateful to **Ephraim Wuensch** whose bold and eclectic artwork graces each lesson of this course. Ephraim is a self-taught artist whose work is part social commentary, part contemporary art. His freestyle stream of consciousness pieces are a window into the creative mind of a contemporary Brooklyn artist straddling the worlds of Hasidic Jewish life within the greater setting of a rapidly gentrifying neighborhood. His seemingly simple lines and use of color belie a sharp wit and creative humor.

Thank you to our Directors of Curriculum, **Rabbis Mordechai Dinerman** and **Naftali Silberberg**, for so generously sharing their expertise on so many levels. To each of you I say: it has been a true pleasure and joy to collaborate with you every step of the way, and I consider myself exceedingly fortunate to reap the rewards of this quintessential dream team. The **Rosh Chodesh Society** is indeed blessed.

Mrs. Malky Bitton, Mrs. Shula Bryski, and **Mrs. Rochel Holzkenner** graciously agreed to lend their expertise and experience—from reviewing curricula, to aiding in general course development, to piloting the course so that others may benefit. We acknowledge their pedagogic and instructional skills and thank them on behalf of the entire **Rosh Chodesh Society**.

Our talented teams have expended numerous hours to bring our materials to production. **Mrs. Rachel Witty** and **Mrs. Ya'akovah Weber** meticulously copyedited and proofread the texts with a great measure of attention and dedication. **Rabbi Zalman Moshe Abraham** created the beautiful book design, and **Mendel Schtroks** is responsible for the wonderful and professional book layout. To **Mrs. Rivki Mockin**, our project manager, your sensibilities in all things book production are commendable and worthy of special mention. I am deeply thankful to all of you. You always rise to the occasion.

We laud our marketing and design team headed by **Rabbi Zalman Moshe Abraham** for their creative vision, attentiveness to the finest of detail, and for producing all our beautiful marketing materials, and we thank **Mrs. Shevi Rivkin** for her special artisanal touch. Great appreciation goes out to **Rabbi Mendy Elishevitz** and **Rabbi Sholom Cohen,** who oversee and ensure the integrity of our cyberspace field.

Special mention must be made regarding our very gifted multimedia team. Thank you, **Mushka Pruss,** for the magnificent PowerPoint presentations—a wonderful asset to each lesson. Having the good fortune to work with **Moshe and Getzy Raskin** of Swish Media, who are simply so good at all things video, is a blessing I'm sure many would wish for.

Many thanks to **Mr. Shimon Leib Jacobs** and to **Mary Stevens** for the printing and distribution of our books. Much gratitude to **Rabbi Mendel Sirota**, who oversees production, shipping, and handling. You always go the extra mile and we acknowledge your efforts.

Kudos to **Mrs. Fraydee Kessler**, an administrator and single-handed project manager *par excellence.* She is much more than her title can ever tell you, and my appreciation for her knows no bounds. Allow me an additional shout-out to **Chana'le Dechter** who multitasks with such grace, integrity and sensitivity, always ensuring seamless fusion between multiple and varied projects. Your contributions are immeasurable.

We acknowledge our Chief of Operations, **Rabbi Levi Kaplan**, a master at everything he does—there are too many tasks and favors to enumerate, but each one is always completed to perfection. Your efforts on behalf of everything **RCS** do not go unnoticed.

The **Rosh Chodesh Society** is enormously grateful for the encouragement of **Rabbi Moshe Kotlarsky,** chairman of the **Rohr Jewish Learning Institute**, and vice chairman of

Merkos L'Inyonei Chinuch—Lubavitch World headquarters. We are fortuitously blessed with the unwavering support of **JLI**'s principal benefactors, **Mr. and Mrs. George and Pamela Rohr** who have staunchly spearheaded and invested in the growth of the organization with an unparalleled commitment. Their dedication is evident and alive within the tens of thousands of Jewish students studying Torah around the globe. May your merit stand you—and all of us—in good stead, and may you reap unbridled blessings all the days of your long, happy, healthy, and auspicious lives.

Heartfelt acclamation to **Mr. and Mrs. Yitzchak and Julie Gniwisch** for their steadfast support and resolute belief in us, always. May the goodness you bring to the world be returned to you ten thousandfold.

JLI's devoted executive board—**Rabbi Chaim Block, Rabbi Hesh Epstein, Rabbi Ronnie Fine, Rabbi Yosef Gansburg, Rabbi Shmuel Kaplan, Rabbi Yisrael Rice,** and **Rabbi Avrohom Sternberg**—give countless hours to the development of **JLI**. Their dedication, commitment, and sage advice have helped the organization grow and flourish.

Rabbi Shmuel Kaplan, chairman of the **Rosh Chodesh Society**, has been instrumental in formulating its vision since its inception, and continues to be a source of guidance as we are blessed to experience tremendous growth within our sisterhood.

The constant progress of **JLI** is a testament to the visionary leadership of our director, **Rabbi Efraim Mintz**, who is never content with the status quo, boldly encourages unbridled innovation and forward thinking, and embodies successful accomplishment. You are an example to many. On this auspicious day, I thank you publicly, both personally and professionally, for this benevolent, outstanding, and truly beneficent opportunity. Directing the **Rosh Chodesh Society** is the calling of my heart and the journey of my soul. It is a gift that keeps on giving eternal blessings. May all who read this be equally blessed. Your merit is great. Thank you for sharing it with me.

The **Rosh Chodesh Society**, **JLI**'s woman's division, was launched on the anniversary of the first *yahrtzeits* of **Rabbi Gavriel Noach** and **Rebbetzin Rivkah Holtzberg**, *H"YD*, devoted Chabad emissaries to Mumbai, India. May the merit of the countless Jewish women who are engaged in these Torah studies serve as a testament to the heroic life they led, and continue to perpetuate their noble deeds.

On behalf of all the individuals who play a role in the **Rosh Chodesh Society**, particularly our affiliates out there on the front lines fulfilling their positions, I offer up a prayer to Almighty G-d: May He actualize the hope of the Jewish nation, as repeatedly expressed by the Lubavitcher Rebbe, of righteous memory, and may we very soon experience the world as it will be, filled with the knowledge of G-d as the waters cover the sea. Amen.

Shluchos! It is solely thanks to you that we will merit the fulfillment of our mandate, *No Jewish Woman Will Be Left Behind*. We could never do it without you. You continue to change the world for the better. Thank you for allowing us to partner with you. You are the heart and soul of the Jewish nation. Indeed, this is the ultimate acknowledgment.

Shaindy Jacobson
Director, **Rosh Chodesh Society**
Brooklyn, New York

Chai (18) Elul, 5776

ROSH CHODESH society FACULTY

UNITED STATES

BIRMINGHAM, AL
Mrs. Frumie Posner
Chabad of Alabama
205.970.0100
cyfposner@aol.com

FOUNTAIN HILLS, AZ
Mrs. Tzipi Lipskier
Chabad of Fountain Hills
480.776.4763
tzipi@jewishfountainhills.com

TUCSON, AZ
Mrs. Feigie Ceitlin
Chabad Lubavitch of Tucson
520.869.4971
FeigieCeitlin@gmail.com

LITTLE ROCK, AR
Mrs. Estie Ciment
Lubavitch of Arkansas
501.221.7940
Estie@arjewishcenter.com

ARCATA, CA
Mrs. Mushkie Cowen
Chabad of Humboldt
412.390.6481
mushkiecowen@gmail.com

BAKERSFIELD, CA
Mrs. Esther Malka Schlanger
Chabad of Bakersfield
661.835.8381
estherm@bak.rr.com

BERKELEY, CA
Mrs. Miriam Chaya Ferris
Chabad of the East Bay
510.684.5292
miriamferris@gmail.com

CALABASAS, CA
Mrs. Shaina Friedman
Chabad of Calabasas
818.222.3838
shaini@jewishcalabasas.com

ENCINO, CA
Mrs. Chana Herzog
Chabad of Encino
818.784.9986
JLI@chabadofthevalley.com

FOLSOM, CA
Mrs. Goldie Grossbaum
Chabad Folsom
916.608.9811
info@jewishfolsom.org

FREMONT, CA
Mrs. Chaya Fuss
Chabad of Fremont
510.300.4090
chaya@chabadfremont.com

FRESNO, CA
Mrs. Chanie Zirkind
Chabad of Fresno
559.432.2770
chabadfresno@sbcglobal.net

GLENDALE, CA
Mrs. Shterny Backman
Chabad of Glendale
818.240.2750
shterny@chabadcenter.org

GOLETA, CA
Mrs. Devorah Loschak
Chabad of S. Barbara
805.324.3584
dloschak@gmail.com

HUNTINGTON BEACH, CA
Mrs. Susha Alperowitz
Chabad of West Orange County
714.846.2285
chabadhb@verizon.net

IRVINE, CA
Mrs. Binie Tenenbaum
Chabad of Irvine
949.786.5000
binie@chabadirvine.org

LAGUNA NIGUEL, CA
Mrs. Kreinie Paltiel
Chabad of Laguna Niguel
949.831.7701
Krein-ic@ChabadLagunaNiguel.com

LONG BEACH, CA
Mrs. Amina Newman
Congregation Lubavitch
562.596.1681
info@longbeachshul.com

LOS ALTOS, CA
Mrs. Nechama Schusterman
Chabad Los Altos
650.858.6990
nechama@bayareafc.org

LOS ANGELES, CA
Mrs. Channa Hecht
Chabad Jewish Center of Brentwood
310.826.4453
channa@chabadbw.com

LOS ANGELES, CA
Mrs. Dvonye Korf
Chabad of Greater Los Feliz
323.660.5177
rabbi@chabadlosfeliz.org

LOS ANGELES, CA
Mrs. Shterny Gurary
Chabad Jewish Center of Hancock Park
323.939.5138
rabbi@jewishhp.com

MALIBU, CA
Mrs. Sarah Cunin
Chabad of Malibu
310.456.6588
sarah@ganmalibu.com

MILL VALLEY, CA
Mrs. Chana Scop
Chabad of Mill Valley
415.419.7296
chanascop@comcast.net

NEWBURY PARK, CA
Mrs. Tzippy Schneerson
Chabad of Newbury Park
805.499.7051
sschneerson@gmail.com

OAKLAND, CA
Mrs. Shulamis Labkowski
Chabad of Oakland
510.545.6770
info@jewishoakland.org

OCEANSIDE, CA
Mrs. Nechama Greenberg
Chabad Jewish Center Oceanside
760.806.7765
Info@jewishoceanside.com

PACIFIC PALISADES, CA
Mrs. Zisi Cunin
Chabad of Pacific Palisades
310.454.7783
info@chabadpalisades.com

PALO ALTO, CA
Mrs. Devory Levin
Chabad Palo Alto
650.561.6013
devory@chabadpaloalto.com

PASADENA, CA
Mrs. Chana Hanoka
Chabad of Pasadena
626.564.8820
hanoka@sbcglobal.net

PLEASANTON, CA
Mrs. Fruma Resnick
Chabad of the Tri-Valley
925.846.0700
Fruma@JewishTriValley.com

RANCHO MIRAGE, CA
Mrs. Chaya Posner
Chabad of Rancho Mirage
760.770.7785
info@chabadrm.com

REDONDO BEACH, CA
Mrs. Sara Mintz
Chabad Jewish Community Center
310.871.5940
saralemintz@aol.com

REDWOOD CITY, CA
Mrs. Ella Potash
Chabad of Redwood City
650.232.0995
ella@jewishredwoodcity.com

SACRAMENTO, CA
Mrs. Dinie Cohen
Chabad of Sacramento
916.455.1400
chabadsac@aol.com

S. DIEGO, CA
Mrs. Leah Fradkin
Chabad of S. Diego
858.547.0076
lfradkin@chasd.org

S. DIEGO, CA
Mrs. Nechama Dina Carlebach
Chabad of Downtown
619.702.8518
Info@chabaddowntown.com

S. FRANCISCO, CA
Mrs. Sara Hecht
RTC-Chabad
415.386.8123
office@rtchabad.org

S. FRANCISCO, CA
Mrs. Mattie Pil
Schneerson Center
415.933.4310
mattieplot@gmail.com

S. MONICA, CA
Mrs. Sara Levitansky
Bais Chabad of Simcha Monica
310.829.5620
soriandisaac@gmail.com

S. MONICA, CA
Mrs. Rivka Rabinowitz
Chabad Living Torah Center
310.394.5699
rabbi@livingtorahcenter.com

S. ROSA, CA
Mrs. Altie Wolvovsky
Chabad Jewish Center
707.577.0277
rabbi@jewishsonoma.com

SEAL BEACH, CA
Mrs. Bluma Marcus
Chabad of Cypress
714.828.1851
shmuelmarcus@yahoo.com

SIMI VALLEY, CA
Mrs. Bassie Gurary
Chabad of Simi Valley
805.577.0573
bassie@chabadsimi.org

TEMECULA, CA
Mrs. Dina Hurwitz
Chabad Jewish Center Temecula Valley
951.813.1401
jewishtemecula@gmail.com

THOUSAND OAKS, CA
Mrs. Shula Bryski
Chabad of Thousand Oaks
805.493.7776
shula@jewishto.org

TOLUCA LAKE, CA
Mrs. Michal Carlebach
Chabad of Toluca Lake
818.308.4118
chabadtl@gmail.com

VACAVILLE, CA
Mrs. Aidel Zaklos
Chabad of Solano County
707.592.5300
rabbi@jewishsolano.com

VENTURA, CA
Mrs. Sarah Miriam Latowicz
Chabad of Ventura
805.658.7441
chabadventura@aol.com

DENVER, CO
Mrs. Elka Popack
Chabad Lubavitch of Colorado
303.780.0537
elkapopack@gmail.com

WESTMINSTER, CO
Mrs. Leah Brackman
Chabad of NW Metro Denver
303.429.5177
Leahbrackman9@gmail.com

GREENWICH, CT
Mrs. Maryashie Deren
Chabad Lubavitch of Greenwich
203.629.9059
info@chabadgreenwich.org

MILFORD, CT
Mrs. Chanie Wilhelm
Chabad Jewish Center of Milford
203.878.4569
chanie@jewishmilford.com

ORANGE, CT
Mrs. Bluma Hecht
Chabad of Orange
203.795.5261
blumahecht@gmail.com

WILMINGTON, DE
Mrs. Rochel Flikshtein
Chabad of Delaware
302.529.9900
Office@ChabadDE.com

BOCA RATON, FL
Mrs. Ahuva New
Chabad of East Boca Raton
561.417.7797
Office@chabadbocabeaches.com

BOCA RATON, FL
Mrs. Rivkah Denburg
Mrs. Chani Bukiet
Chabad of Boca Raton
561.994.6257
ikaden@aol.com

BOYNTON BEACH, FL
Mrs. Dina Ciment
Chabad of Boynton
561.732.4633
ciments@gmail.com

BRADENTON, FL
Mrs. Chanie Bukiet
Chabad of Bradenton and Lakewood Ranch
941.752.3030
Chanie@chabadofbradenton.com

FORT LAUDERDALE, FL
Mrs. Rochel Holzkenner
Chabad of Las Olas
954.224.7162
rochelholzkenner@gmail.com

JUPITER, FL
Mrs. Chaya Sarah Barash
Chabad Jewish Center of Jupiter
561.694.6950
csbarash@yahoo.com

LAKE MARY, FL
Mrs. Chanshy Majesky
Chabad-Lubavitch of North Orlando
407.878.3011
chanshy@JewishNorthOrlando.com

LAKE WORTH, FL
Mrs. Leah Rosenfeld
Chabad Lake Worth
561.649.8468
Chabadlakeworth@gmail.com

LAKELAND, FL
Mrs. Libby Lazaros
Chabad of Lakeland
863.510.5968
mendel@chabadlakeland.org

MIAMI, FL
Mrs. Chana Gopin
Chabad at Midtown
305.573.9995
info@maormiami.org

MIAMI, FL
Mrs. Gutal Fellig
Chabad of South Dade
305.445.5444
info@chabadmiami.com

MIAMI BEACH, FL
Mrs. Chani Katz
Chabad House in Miami Beach
305.505.9065
rabbi@mbjewish.com

MIAMI BEACH, FL
Mrs. Tzippy Mann
Chabad of Venetian & Sunset Islands
305.674.8400
tzippymann@gmail.com

PALM BEACH, FL
Mrs. Hindel Levitin
Chabad of Northern Palm Beach Island
561.659.3884
hindelle@gmail.com

PALM HARBOR, FL
Mrs. Mushky Adler
Chabad of Pinellas County
248.305.0462
emailmushka@gmail.com

PALMETTO BAY, FL
Mrs. Chani Gansburg
Chabad of Palmetto Bay
786.282.0413
chabadpalmettobay@gmail.com

PUNTA GORDA, FL
Mrs. Sheina Jacobson
Chabad of Charlotte County
941.833.3381
chabadpg@yahoo.com

ROYAL PALM BEACH, FL
Mrs. Leah Schtroks
Chabad of Royal Palm Beach
561.795.1534
rabbizevis@gmail.com

S. PETERSBURG, FL
Mrs. Chaya Korf
Chabad Jewish Center
727.344.4900
chaya@chabadsp.com

SARASOTA, FL
Mrs. Sara Steinmetz
Chabad of Sarasota
941.925.0770
steinmetz.sara@gmail.com

SUNNY ISLES BEACH, FL
Mrs. Chanie Kaller
Chabad Russian Center
305.803.5315
Rabbi@chabadrc.org

SURFSIDE, FL
Mrs. Chani Lipskar
The Shul of Bal Harbour
305.868.1411
info@theshul.org

TAMPA, FL
Mrs. Sulha Dubrowski
Chabad of Tampa Bay
813.963.2317
lamplightersd@gmail.com

VALRICO, FL
Mrs. Tzippy Rubashkin
Chabad of Brandon
813.571.8100
tzipsor@gmail.com

WESLEY CHAPEL, FL
Mrs. Chanie Yarmush
Chabad at Wiregrass
813.731.4435
Ceedee15@aol.com

ATLANTA, GA
Mrs. Dassie New
Chabad of Georgia
404.843.2464 ext.102
office@chabadga.com

ATLANTA, GA
Mrs. Leah Sollish
Mrs. Dena Schusterman
Chabad In-town
404.898.0434
leah@chabadintown.org

KENNESAW, GA
Mrs. Nechami Charytan
Chabad Jewish Center
678.460.7702
info@jewishwestcobb.com

BOISE, ID
Mrs. Esther M. Lifshitz
Chabad Lubavitch of Idaho
208.841.9927
esther@jewishidaho.com

CHICAGO, IL
Mrs. Chaya Epstein
Women to Women
773.875.9147
w2wchaya@gmail.com

CHICAGO, IL
Mrs. Dinie Cohen
Jewish Women's Group
773.262.1381
ndcohen@sbcglobal.net

DEERFIELD, IL
Mrs. Dena Brody
Chabad House
305.335.9770
denabrody1@gmail.com

GLENVIEW, IL
Mrs. Sara Benjaminson
Rohr Chabad Center of Glenview
847.998.0770
Chabad@ChabadofGlenview.com

HIGHLAND PARK, IL
Mrs. Michla Schanowitz
North Suburban Chabad
847.433.1567
yschanow@sbcglobal.net

NORTHBROOK, IL
Mrs. Esther Rochel Moscowitz
Lubavitch Chabad of Northbrook
847.564.8770
info@chabadnorthbrook.com

DAVENPORT, IA
Mrs. Chana Cadaner
Chabad Lubavitch of the Quad Cities
563.355.1065
Chana@Chabadquadcities.com

IOWA CITY, IA
Mrs. Chaya Blesofsky
Chabad Lubavitch of Iowa City
319.358.1323
chabadiowa@msn.com

OVERLAND PARK, KS
Mrs. Blumah Wineberg
Neshei Chabad of KC
913.649.4852
nesheichabad@gmail.com

LEXINGTON, KY
Mrs. Shoshi Litvin
Chabad of the Bluegrass
502.576.0392
chabadofthebluegrass@gmail.com

METAIRIE, LA
Mrs. Chanie Nemes
Chabad Jewish Center
504.957.4987
chanienemes@gmail.com

ANNAPOLIS, MD
Mrs. Hindy Light
Chabad of Anne Arundel County
443.321.9859
hindy@chabadaac.com

BALTIMORE, MD
Mrs. Rochelle Kaplan
Aleph Learning Institute
410.486.2666 ext.2
alephjli@gmail.com

BEL AIR, MD
Mrs. Fraida Malka Schusterman
Chabad of Harford County
443.353.9718
Chabad@HarfordJewish.com

COLUMBIA, MD
Mrs. Chaya Sufrin
Lubavitch Center of Howard County
443.474.0340
rabbi@chabadclarksville.org

GAITHERSBURG, MD
Mrs. Chana Raichik
Chabad Upper Montgomery County
301.537.0068
chana@ourshul.org

OLNEY, MD
Mrs. Devorah Stolik
Chabad of Olney
301.660.6770
info@jewisholney.com

OWINGS MILLS, MD
Mrs. Chanie Katsenelenbogen
chabad Owings Mills
410.356.5156
chanie@chabadom.com

POTOMAC, MD
Mrs. Chana Kaplan
Chabad of the Village
301.433.4524
villagechabad@gmail.com

POTOMAC, MD
Mrs. Sarale Bluming
Chabad of Potomac
240.621.0770
sara@chabadpotomac.com

SILVER SPRING, MD
Mrs. Chaya Wolvovsky
Chabad of Silver Spring
301.593.1117
chayawolvovsky@gmail.com

CHESTNUT HILL, MA
Mrs. Grunie Uminer
Chabad at Chestnut Hill
617.738.9770
grunie@chabadch.com

NATICK, MA
Mrs. Chanie Fogelman
Chabad Center of Natick
508.202.2283
education@chabadnatick.com

PEABODY, MA
Mrs. Raizel Schusterman
Chabad of Peabody
978.977.9111
raizel@jewishpeabody.com

STOUGHTON, MA
Mrs. Chana Gurkow
Shaloh House
781.344.6334
rabbi@shalohhouse.com

SUDBURY, MA
Mrs. Shayna Freeman
Chabad Center of Sudbury
978.443.0110
info@chabadsudbury.com

WELLESLEY, MA
Mrs. Geni Bleich
Wellesley Weston Chabad House
781.239.1076
JewishWomenRgr8@aol.com

COMMERCE, MI
Mrs. Estie Greenberg
Chabad Jewish Center of Commerce
248.363.3644
estie@jewishcommerce.org

SOUTHFIELD, MI
Mrs. Tzippy Misholovin
FREE of Michigan
248.569.8514
free.michigan@yahoo.com

WEST BLOOMFIELD, MI
Mrs. Itty Shemtov
The Shul
248.788.4000
itty@theshul.net

MINNETONKA, MN
Ms. Rivkie Grossbaum
Chabad Minneapolis
952.929.9922
rivka@ChabadMinneapolis.com

S. PAUL, MN
Mrs. Nechama Bendet
Chabad Lubavitch of Greater S. Paul
651.998.9298
jewishspaul@gmail.com

KANSAS CITY, MO
Mrs. Chana'le Itkin
Chabad on the Plaza
816.645.6610
chana@plazachabad.com

S. LOUIS, MO
Mrs. Shiffy Landa
Chabad of Greater St. Louis
314.725.0400
chaim@showmechabad.com

BOZEMAN, MT
Mrs. Chavie Bruk
Chabad-Lubavitch of Montana
406.585.8770
chavs84@yahoo.com

MISSOULA, MT
Mrs. Shayna Nash
Chabad Lubavitch of Missoula
406.529.3196
berrynash@gmail.com

MANCHESTER, NH
Mrs. Shternie Krinsky
Lubavitch of New Hampshire
603.647.0204
shterniekrinsky@gmail.com

CHERRY HILL, NJ
Mrs. Dinie Mangel
Chabad Lubavitch in Cherry Hill
856.874.1500
Dinie@TheChabadCenter.org

CLINTON, NJ
Mrs. Rachel Kornfeld
Chabad of Hunterdon County
908.238.9002
rachel@jewishhunterdon.com

FRANKLIN LAKES, NJ
Mrs. Mimi Kaplan
Chabad of NW Bergen County – Franklin Lakes
201.848.0449
kaplanmimi@gmail.com

FREEHOLD, NJ
Mrs. Zisi Bernstein
Chabad of Freehold
732.972.3687
zisinj@gmail.com

HOBOKEN, NJ
Mrs. Shaindel Schapiro
Chabad Hoboken
201.386.5222
chabadhoboken@gmail.com

MONTVILLE, NJ
Mrs. Chaya Schera Spalter
Chabad of Montville
973.727.8824
Chabadmontville@aol.com

MORRISTOWN, NJ
Mrs. Gani Goodman
Morristown RCA
917.860.0146
jdomber@gmail.com

RANDOLPH, NJ
Mrs. Chava Bekhor
Chabad of Randolph
973.895.3070
info@chabadrandolph.com

TOMS RIVER, NJ
Mrs. Chanie Gourarie
Chabad Toms River
732.349.4199
chanie@chabadtomsriver.com

VINELAND, NJ
Mrs. Nechama Rapoport
Chabad of Cumberland County
856.207.3797
yohama1@verizon.net

WEST ORANGE, NJ
Mrs. Altie Kasowitz
Lubavitch Center
973.486.2362
altiekas@yahoo.com

WOODCLIFF LAKE, NJ
Mrs. Hindy Drizin
Valley Chabad
201.476.0157
hindy@valleychabad.org

LAS CRUCES, NM
Mrs. Chenchie Schmukler
Chabad of Las Cruces
575.524.1330
chenchie@ymail.com

BEDFORD HILLS, NY
Mrs. Sara Wolf
Chabad of Bedford & Pound Ridge Towns
914.666.6065
sara@chabadbedford.com

BRONX, NY
Mrs. Sorah Shemtov
Chabad Lubavitch of Riverdale
718.549.1100 ext. 15
sorahshmtv@gmail.com

BRONXVILLE, NY
Mrs. Mushka Deitsch
Chabad of Bronxville
347.623.0449
mushka@jewishbronxville.com

BROOKLYN, NY
Mrs. Chana'le Levin
Chabad of Ditmas Park
347.850.2255
ChabadofDitmasPark@gmail.com

BROOKLYN, NY
Mrs. Chanel Lipskier
Mrs. Dvora Lakein
The Beis Medrash Women's Circle
718.778.6712
WC@thebeismedrash.com

BROOKLYN, NY
Mrs. Devorah Marosov
Chabad of Midwood
718.338.3324
dmarsow@gmail.com

BROOKLYN, NY
Mrs. Esther Abramowitz
Chabad-Lubavitch of Clinton Hill
718.974.9472
esther@greenechabad.com

BROOKLYN, NY
Mrs. Esther Winner
Chabad Neshama
718.946.9833 ext.104
estherwinner@gmail.com

BROOKLYN, NY
Mrs. Sarah Hecht
Chabad of Park Slope
718.965.9836
shconquer@aol.com

BROOKLYN, NY
Mrs. Tzippy Vigler
Meorot Torah Center
718.677.0030
tzippy@meorotcenter.com

CEDARHURST, NY
Mrs. Chana Wolowik
Sara Blau
Chabad of the Five Towns
516.295.2478
chanie@chabad5towns.com

FLUSHING, NY
Mrs. Chanie Zalmanov
Chabad of Eastern Queens
718.464.0778
chaniezalmanov@gmail.com

FOREST HILLS, NY
Mrs. Mushky Mendelson
Congregation Machane Chodosh
347.867.8672
rabbi@machanechodosh.org

GREAT NECK, NY
Mrs. Chanie Geisinsky
Chabad of Great Neck
516.528.6033
cgeisinsky@gmail.com

MAMARONECK, NY
Mrs. Chana Silberstein
Jewish Women's Circle
914.834.8000
chana@jewishlarchmont.com

NEW YORK, NY
Mrs. Chana Paris
Chabad of Tribeca
212.566.6764
info@chabadoftribeca.com

NEW YORK, NY
Mrs. Chanie Krasnianski
Chabad Upper East Side
212.717.4613
ckrasnianski@gmail.com

NEW YORK, NY
Mrs. Devora Wilhelm
Chabad Young Professionals UES
347.451.4375
chabadyp@gmail.com

NEW YORK, NY
Mrs. Frumie Weitman
Chabad Jewish Latin Center
646.678.3569
jewishlatincenternyc@gmail.com

NEW YORK, NY
Mrs. Gillie Shanowitz
New York Hebrew
646.573.6773
gillie@nychebrewschool.org

NEW YORK, NY
Mrs. Mushka Zaklos
Chabad of Battery Park
646.770.3636
jewishbpc@gmail.com

NEW YORK, NY
Mrs. Rachel Benchimol
Aleph Learning
646.827.9181
info@alephlearning.org

NEW YORK, NY
Mrs. Raizy Metzger
Upper Midtown Chabad
212.758.3770
raizymetzger@yahoo.com

ROCHESTER, NY
Mrs. Chany Mochkin
Chabad Lubavitch of Rochester
585.981.0477
chanymo@yahoo.com

STONY BROOK, NY
Mrs. Chanie Cohen
Neshei Chabad Woman's Club
631.585.521
chanie@chabadsb.com

SUFFERN, NY
Mrs. Esty Weber
NCFJE
443.418.4336
Estherweber7@gmail.com

CINCINNATI, OH
Mrs. Chana Mangel
Chabad Jewish Center
513.793.5200
office@chabadba.com

CLEVELAND, OH
Mrs. Estie Marozov
Friendship Circle
216.377.3000
RabbiYossi@ChabadofCleveland.com

DAYTON, OH
Mrs. Devorah Leah Mangel
Chabad of Greater Dayton
937.643.0770
chabad@chabaddayton.com

NEW ALBANY, OH
Mrs. Esther Kaltmann
Chabad of Columbus
614.610.4293
esther.kaltmann@sbcglobal.net

SALEM, OR
Mrs. Fruma Perlstein
Chabad Jewish Center of Salem
503.383.9569
Fruma@chabadsalem.com

ALLENTOWN, PA
Mrs. Devorah Halperin
Chabad of the Lehigh Valley
610.351.6511
Rabbi@chabadlehighvalley.com

FORT WASHINGTON, PA
Mrs. Devorah Leah Deitsch
Lubavitch of Montgomery County
215.591.9310
devorah@jewishmc.com

MERION STATION, PA
Mrs. Michal Sherman
Chabad of the Main Line
610.660.9900
michal@chabadmainline.org

NEWTOWN, PA
Mrs. Rosie Weinstein
Lubavitch of Bucks County
215.497.9925
rosie@jewishcenter.info

PITTSBURGH, PA
Mrs. Chani Altein
Chabad of Pittsburgh
412.421.3561
jli@chabadpgh.com

RYDAL, PA
Mrs. Nechama Dina Gurevitz
Chabad Lubavitch Jewish Center
267.536.5757
zusheg@gmail.com

STATE COLLEGE, PA
Mrs. Miri Gourarie
Chabad of the Undergrad
814.409.8130
mirigourarie@gmail.com

STATE COLLEGE, PA
Mrs. Sarah Meretsky
Chabad of Penn State
814.861.8063
sarahitameretsky@comcast.net

ASHVILLE, SC
Mrs. Chana Susskind
Chabad House of Ashville
828.505.0746
chana@chabadasheville.org

COLUMBIA, SC
Mrs. Devorah Leah Marrus
The Chabad-Alef House
803.237.6084
devorahld@gmail.com

MYRTLE BEACH, SC
Mrs. Leah Aizenmen
Chabad of Myrtle Beach
843.448.0035
laizenman@gmail.com

MEMPHIS, TN
Mrs. Rivky Klein
Chabad Lubavitch of Tennessee
901.754.0404
Info@JewishMemphis.com

NASHVILLE, TN
Mrs. Esther Tiechtel
Chabad of Nashville
615.646.5750
rabbi@chabadnashville.com

ARLINGTON, TX
Mrs. Risha Gurevitch
Chabad of Arlington
817.451.1171
rishi@arlingtonchabad.org

AUSTIN, TX
Mrs. Mussy Levertov
Chabad Young Professionals
512.905.2778
Mendyaustin@gmail.com

BELLAIRE, TX
Mrs. Esty Zaklikofsky
The Shul of Bellaire
713.484.9887
estyzak@gmail.com

DALLAS, TX
Mrs. Michal Shapiro
Chabad of Dallas
972.818.0770
moshenaparstek@gmail.com

FORT WORTH, TX
Mrs. Chana Tovah Mandel
Chabad of Fort Worth
817.263.7701
Cgi@chabadfortworth.com

HOUSTON, TX
Mrs. Leah Marinovsky
Chabad Lubavitch
713.541.1774
leahfeige2@aim.com

HOUSTON, TX
Mrs. Rochel Lazaroff
Chabad at Rice
713.522.2004
Rochel@aishelhouse.org

S. ANTONIO, TX
Mrs. Rivkie Block
Chabad Lubavitch
210.492.1085
chabadsa@sbcglobal.net

SALT LAKE CITY, UT
Mrs. Sheina Zippel
Chabad Lubavitch of Utah
801.414.3377
sheina@jewishutah.com

BURLINGTON, VT
Mrs. Draizy Junik
Chabad of Vermont
802.658.5770
chabad@chabadvt.org

NORFOLK, VA
Mrs. Rashi Brashevitzky
Chabad of Tidewater
757.616.0770
Rabbilevi@chabadoftidewater.com

MERCER ISLAND, WA
Mrs. Devorah Kornfeld
Chabad of Mercer Island
206.679.9117
y-kornfeld2@yahoo.com

OLYMPIA, WA
Mrs. Chava Edelman
Chabad of Olympia
360.584.4306
info@jewisholympia.com

SPOKANE, WA
Mrs. Chaya Sarah Hahn
Chabad of Spokane
509.443.0770
rabbihahn@gmail.com

VANCOUVER, WA
Mrs. Tzivie Greenberg
Chabad Jewish Center
360.326.5923
info@jewishclarkcounty.com

KENOSHA, WI
Mrs. Rivkie Wilschanski
Chabad of Kenosha
262.359.0770
rabbitzali@jewishkenosha.com

MADISON, WI
Mrs. Henya Matusof
Rohr Chabad House at University of Wisconsin-Madison
608.257.1757
Info@jewishuwmadison.com

MEQUON, WI
Mrs. Dinie Rapoport
Center for Jewish Life
262.242.2235
dinie@chabadmequon.com

US VIRGIN ISLANDS

S. THOMAS
Mrs. Henya Federman
Chabad Lubavitch of the Virgin Islands
340.714.2770
henya@jewishvirginislands.com

AUSTRALIA

ROSE BAY, NSW
Mrs. Henya Milecki
South Head Synagogue
61.4.2361.3770
henyam@me.com

SYDNEY, NSW
Mrs. Sara-Tova Yaffe
CBD Chabad
61.4.2247.0655
saratova613@gmail.com

EAST ST KILDA, VIC
Mrs. Sara Rosenfeld
Beis Chabad Ohel Devorah
61.3.9525.9014
rivkah.groner@gmail.com

BELGIUM

BRUSSELS
Mrs. Nehama Tawil
EJCC
32.2.231.1770
ntawil@ejcc.eu

BRUSSELS
Mrs. Shulamit Pinson
Ohel Menachem
32.47.621.7445
info@ganihai.com

EDEGEM, ANTWERPEN
Mrs. Chaya Hertz
Chai Center
32.3.288.7970
chajah@gmail.com

BRAZIL

MANAUS
Mrs. Dvorah Lea Raichman
Chabad-Lubavitch of Manaus
55.92.3088.3302
Zagudeby@hotmail.com

S. PAULO
Mrs. Rivka Rosenfeld
Sinagoga Beit Menachem
55.11.3816.6216
rivkyrosenfeld@hotmail.com

S. PAULO
Mrs. Sarah Steinmetz
Beit Chabad Central
55.11.3081.3081
sarah.a.steinmetz@gmail.com

CANADA

RICHMOND, BC
Mrs. Chanie Baitelman
Chabad of Richmond
604.277.6427
admin@chabadrichmond.com

VANCOUVER, BC
Mrs. Chaya Rosenfeld
Lubavitch of British Columbia
604.266.1313
esti@lubavitchbc.com

VANCOUVER, BC
Mrs. Malky Bitton
Chabad of Downtown
778.688.1273
malky@chabadcitycentre.com

HAMILTON, ON
Mrs. Shaina Rosenfeld
Chabad Lubavitch Hamilton
905.529.7458
shaina@chabadhamilton.com

MAPLE, ON
Mrs. Toby Bernstein
Chabad Romano Centre
905.303.1880
chabad@chabadrc.org

OTTAWA, ON
Mrs. Devora Caytak
Jewish Youth Library of Ottawa
613.729.1619
Dev18@sympatico.ca

S. CATHARINES, ON
Mrs. Perla Zaltzman
Chabad at Brock
905.401.6281
perla@Jewishniagara.com

THORNHILL, ON
Mrs. Chanah Leah Beckerman
Chabad at York
905.771.6359
bekermans@gmail.com

THORNHILL, ON
Mrs. Chanie Hildeshaim
Chabad Russian Center of Thornhill Woods
905.326.9258
chanie@jewishthornhillwoods.org

THORNHILL, ON
Mrs. Faygie Kaplan
Chabad @ Flamingo
905.763.4040
faygie@chabadflamingo.com

THORNHILL, ON
Mrs. Goldie Plotkin
Chabad Lubavitch of Markham
905.886.0420
rabbi@chabadmarkham.org

TORONTO, ON
Mrs. Chana Gansburg
Chabad on the Avenue
416.546.8770
chana@chabadavenue.com

TORONTO, ON
Mrs. Nechama Dina Jacobson
Mrs. Mushky Blau
JRCC West Thornhill
416.902.9254
ndjacobson@rogers.com

TORONTO, ON
Mrs. Rivka Gansburg
Chabad Lubavitch of York Mills
416.551.9391
rivky@chabadyorkmills.com

TORONTO, ON
Mrs. Yehudis Steiner
Uptown Chabad
416.635.9696
yehudissteiner@gmail.com

WATERLOO, ON
Mrs. Rivky Goldman
Chabad Lubavitch of the Waterloo Region
519.725.4289
rmg@jewishwaterloo.com

WHITBY, ON
Mrs. Chana Borenstein
Chabad Jewish Centre of Durham Region
905.493.9007
info@jewishdurham.com

MONTREAL, QC
Mrs. Chanie Gansbourg
Chabad of Old Montreal
514.907.8778
chabadofoldmtl@gmail.com

MONTREAL, QC
Mrs. Rashi Weiss
Chabad Student Centre
514.845.4443
rashi@chabadmcgill.com

MONTREAL, QC
Mrs. Simcha Fine
Chabad Zichron Kedoshim
514.738.3434
simchafine@gmail.com

MONTREAL, QC
Mrs. Zeldie Treitel
Montreal Torah Center
514.739.0770
zeldie@themtc.com

VILLE S. LAURENT, QC
Mrs. Leah Silberstein
Chabad Ville S. Laurent
514.747.1199
info@chabadvsl.com

CAYMAN ISLANDS
GRAND CAYMAN
Mrs. Rikal Pewzner
Chabad Cayman
717.798.1040
rikal@jewishcayman.com

CHINA
PUDONG
Mrs. Nechama Greenberg
Chabad of Pudong
86.21.1780.0791
nechamieg@gmail.com

DENMARK
COPENHAGEN
Mrs. Rochel Loewenthal
ChabaDanmark
45.3316.1850
Info@chabad.dk

FRANCE
MARSEILLE
Mrs. Vivi (Rivky) Altabé
Beth Habad Marseille 8ème
33.6.11.600.305
loubavitch13008@gmail.com

PARIS
Mrs. Mushky Lachkar
Habad Bercy 13
33.6.63.025.430
mushky92@gmail.com

PAU
Mrs. Shayna Matusof
Habad des Pyrenees-Atlantiques
33.6.22.107.549
habadpyrenees@gmail.com

GUATEMALA
GUATEMALA CITY
Mrs. Yael Pelman
Chabad of Guatemala
718.504.7344
yaell@hotmail.com

ISRAEL
JERUSALEM
Mrs. Chana Canterman
Chabad Center of Talbiya
972.54.682.3737
chabadtalbiya@gmail.com

ITALY
FIRENZE
Mrs. Sonia Wolvovsky
Chabad of Tuscany
39.38.9595.2034
jewishtuscany@gmail.com

RUSSIAN FEDERATION
MOSCOW
Mrs. Rivky Wilansky
Chabad of Moscow
7.495.645.5000
doamitzvah@gmail.com

SOUTH AFRICA
SEA POINT, CAPE TOWN
Mrs. Avigail Popack
Chabad Center of Cape Town
27.21.434.3740
avipopack@gmail.com

SWEDEN
MALMÖ
Mrs. Reizel Kesselman
Chabad Malmo
46.40.979.358
chabadmalmo@gmail.com

SWITZERLAND

LUGANO
Mrs. Yuti Kantor
Chabad Lugano
41.91.921.3720
Yuti@jewishlugano.com

LUZERN
Mrs. Rivky Drukman
Chabad of Central Switzerland
41.41.361.1770
Info@ChabadLuzern.com

UNITED KINGDOM

BIRMINGHAM, ENGLAND
Mrs. Rivky Cheruff
Chabad on Campus Birmingham
44.78.05092236
dercheruff@gmail.com

EDGWARE, MIDDX, ENGLAND
Mrs. Sarah Jacobs
Lubavitch of Edgware
44.20.8905.4141
sarahjacobs@loe.org.uk

EDGWARE, MIDDX, ENGLAND
Mrs. Shterna Sudak
Lubavitch Foundation
44.20.8800.0022
Shternasudak@yahoo.com

ILFORD, ESSEX, ENGLAND
Mrs. Devorah Sufrin
Chabad Lubavitch Centres Essex
44.20.8554.1624
mrssufrin@chabadilford.co.uk

LEEDS, ENGLAND
Mrs. Dabrushy Pink
Chabad Lubavitch of Leeds
44.11.3266.3311
Dpink57@gmail.com

LONDON, ENGLAND
Mrs. Chai Cohen
Chabad-Lubavitch of Shoreditch
44.77.7261.2661
cohenchai@gmail.com

LONDON, ENGLAND
Mrs. Devora Lew
Chabad of Bloomsbury - Central London
44.20.7060.9770
info@bloomsburychabad.org

LONDON, ENGLAND
Mrs. Devorah Leah Weisz
Chabad of Hampstead Village
44.79.7652.2807
Shulinhampstead@gmail.com

LONDON, ENGLAND
Mrs. Hadasa Korer
Chabad Lubavitch of Islington
44.20.7688.0169
mkorer@gmail.com

LONDON, ENGLAND
Mrs. Kezi Levin
Brondesbury Park Synagogue
44.20.8451.0091
kezi@bark.org

MANCHESTER, ENGLAND
Mrs. Shaina Cohen
Lchaim Chabad Manchester
44.16.1792.6335
Shaina@Lchaim.org.uk

WESTMINSTER, LONDON, ENGLAND
Mrs. Chana Kalmenson
Chabad of Belgravia
44.75.8592.0195
jewishbelgravia@gmail.com

URUGUAY

MONTEVIDEO
Mrs. Musya Shemtov
Beit Jabad Uruguay
598.2709.3444
rmusyashemtov@gmail.com

VENEZUELA

CARACAS
Mrs. Chani Rosenblum
Hogar Jabad Lubavitch
58.212.264.7011
chaniros1@gmail.com

JEWISH LEARNING INSTITUTE

THE JEWISH LEARNING MULTIPLEX
Brought to you by the Rohr Jewish Learning Institute

In fulfillment of the mandate of the Lubavitcher Rebbe, of blessed memory,
whose leadership guides every step of our work,
the mission of the Rohr Jewish Learning Institute is to transform
Jewish life and the greater community through the study of Torah,
connecting each Jew to our shared heritage of Jewish learning.

While our flagship program remains the cornerstone of our organization,
JLI is proud to feature additional divisions catering to specific populations,
in order to meet a wide array of educational needs.

THE ROHR JEWISH LEARNING INSTITUTE,
a subsidiary of *Merkos L'Inyonei Chinuch*,
is the adult education arm of the Chabad-Lubavitch Movement.

TORAH STUDIES

Torah Studies provides a rich and nuanced encounter with the weekly Torah reading.

MYSHIUR
TALMUD LEARNING INITIATIVE

MyShiur courses are designed to assist students in developing the skills needed to study Talmud independently.

SINAI SCHOLARS SOCIETY
IN PARTNERSHIP WITH CHABAD ON CAMPUS

This rigorous fellowship program invites select college students to explore the fundamentals of Judaism.

JLI TEENS
YOUNG SMART JEWISH
IN PARTNERSHIP WITH CTEEN: CHABAD TEEN NETWORK

Jewish teens forge their identity as they engage in Torah study, social interaction, and serious fun.

ROSHCHODESH society

The Rosh Chodesh Society gathers Jewish women together once a month for intensive textual study.

TORAHCafé

TorahCafe.com provides an exclusive selection of top-rated Jewish educational videos.

BRILLIANT LEARNING, NATURALLY.
National JEWISH RETREAT

This yearly event rejuvenates mind, body, and spirit with a powerful synthesis of Jewish learning and community.

The LAND & THE SPIRIT ISRAEL EXPERIENCE

Participants delve into our nation's rich past while exploring the Holy Land's relevance and meaning today.

PEDAGOGY · CURRICULUM · MARKETING
JLI ACADEMY

Select affiliates are invited to partner with peers and noted professionals, as leaders of innovation and excellence.

מכון שמואל

THE SAMI ROHR RESEARCH INSTITUTE

Machon Shmuel is an institute providing Torah research in the service of educators worldwide.

NOTES

NOTES

NOTES